THE PASSION

By

Dr. Bree M. Keyton, Th.D., D.C.E.

Black Forest Press
San Diego, California
February, 2004

First Edition, Fourth Printing

THE PASSION

By

Dr. Bree M. Keyton, Th.D., D.C.E.

PUBLISHED IN THE UNITED STATES OF AMERICA
BY
BLACK FOREST PRESS
P.O. Box 6342
Chula Vista, CA 919909-6342

Cover Design: Monica Nagy
Cover Set Up: Aurora Zhivago
Editor: Dahk Knox

Printed in the United States of America
Library of Congress
Cataloging in Publication

ISBN: 1-58275-042-4

Table of Contents

Table of Contents Part One: *WHAT IS THE PASSION?*

Table of Contents Part Two: *THORNS*

Table of Contents Part Three: *THE BLOOD*

Introduction

The passion of the Messiah is an event in history that stands alone. In the following pages I will endeavor to bring this wonderful story to you in a personal way. In May of 1993, God gave me a vision of Yahshua Messiah (Jesus Christ) receiving His stripes before He went to the cross. It was a horrible, bloody vision that shook me to my foundation. The sight of Jesus Christ's blood and flesh being ripped and flayed, pieces of skin and blood exploding everywhere, was more than I could bear. I will never be the same after "seeing" this event. The LORD spoke to me and told me to write a song, and He would heal His people. I wrote a song with thirty-nine whip cracks in it, and the LORD has been faithful to heal His people. I debuted it at a crusade two weeks later and many were sovereignly healed that night by God's own hand.

The next day I was praising and worshiping my heavenly Father for His faithfulness when He gave me the directive to write the songs "*Nails*" and "*Thorns*." I said, "LORD, what do the nails and thorns represent?" The subsequent three-year journey to find the answer to this question was filled with prayer, fasting, waiting, and the divine influence working patience in my heart.

I received the songs and the book, *Stripes, Nails, Thorns and The Blood*, through revelation. Many people have been healed and delivered through these songs, and you will treasure them too. My husband likes to listen to them while driving, to get free from the daily oppressions of life. It is such a privilege to uncover the truths of biblical healing and deliverance, so that many may walk in victory, marching together to defeat the enemy of our souls.

This book is Part One of a three part book series. Part Two, to be released next year, will be entitled *Stripes*. It is a revelation of Jesus' stripes that heal us. Part Three will be *Nails*, explaining how the nails Jesus took in His hands and feet delivered us.

i

Bree's musical CD received nationwide airplay for several years. It is a powerful audio, dramatic work embracing everything Jesus accomplished on the cross.

Scripture references are *KJV* and *Strong's Exhaustive Concordance*, unless otherwise specified.

Part One

WHAT IS
THE PASSION?

Chapter One
What Does *The Passion* Mean?

A few years ago, a mother and her little boy were swimming in the ocean when a shark suddenly attacked the child. The mother leaped through the waves and pounded the shark with her fists until it finally let go of the boy and swam away. Extreme danger caused this mother to rise above the limits of the ordinary into the rarified air of the extraordinary. The child was saved because of a mother's violent act of selfless love. Who else would attack a shark with only fists for weapons?

When human emotions are kicked into high gear, we have a phenomenon known as PASSION. Occasionally, the news will carry a story of an individual lifting a heavy car off someone trapped beneath? Impossible? Great passion and compassion lifts us above what is possible, to soar to the heights of human potential.

Recently, a Congressional Medal of Honor recipient gave an account of his selfless act of courage. As a navy corpsman in Viet Nam, he was giving medical treatment to a dozen injured men, when grenades were suddenly thrown into the tent. He threw them outside as fast as he could, but the last one rolled around the room so long that he felt his only chance to save the others was to fall on it. He laid on it for a few seconds, and then bravely threw it outside. While in the air it exploded. The power from the blast went the other way and everyone survived the attack. A noble purpose can lift an average man into superhuman exploits. The desire to protect someone we love can be defined as passion. The ability to do extraordinary deeds because of our passion comes from an unknown source within ourselves, and is still a mystery. Perhaps it is the divine spark within us. We are, after all, more than just flesh and blood.

WHAT IS THE PASSION?

Webster's defines PASSION as "intense or violent emotion." Compassion, according to *Webster's,* involves sympathetic concern for the suffering of another, and to show mercy.

Some of the most memorable and moving stories throughout history depict a love so great, that death is not too great a price to pay to save another. Nothing has ever been more violent than the torture and death of Jesus, the Christ, of Nazareth. His PASSION was more than just sacrifice, it was the defining moment in history, occurring nearly two-thousand years ago. That moment, when He forgave His enemies, as He gave up His life nailed to a cross, stands alone in history. Never before has one man died for so many.

During His life He spoke of a "greater love," laying down one's life for a friend, as being the best a man could do to prove His love. This He demonstrated for us as He suffered on the cross. [1]

PASSION is a verb used in the book of Acts meaning to experience a sensation or impression, usually painful. [2] *Vine's,* a dictionary of biblical words, defines PASSION: "to suffer."

Can you think of a time in your life when you suffered for another person by keeping silent? Perhaps you have been accused of something you did not do. There have been many brave men and women who refused to betray one another during interrogations and wars all throughout history.

Chapter Two
The Greatest Love Story Ever Told

Many stories down through time have a tragic theme of star-crossed lovers, with a love so great that only death can part them. We are moved in the depth of our souls by such stories as *Romeo and Juliet*, in which two passionate lovers die for love. The shock of their sacrifice causes their families to reconcile their hatred and make peace.

Passion can also generate the opposite of love: hatred. Passionate hate generates many headlines. Jealousy, envy, fear, shame and hatred are all strong motivators. Such passionate emotions can lead to extremes, acted out through genocide and world wars.

Strong emotions can bypass the reasoning center, resulting in actions not tempered by reason, or restrained by normal inhibitions. Many foolish things have been done in the heat of passion. No one is exempt from its force. Strong emotions can produce positive or negative results.

LOVE IS STRONGER THAN HATE! Love turns the world upside down, and makes life worth living! Passionate love is an individual act that does not necessarily require the action of others. It is *for* others. The movie, ***The Passion of Christ***, depicts the powerful events surrounding Jesus Christ's death and resurrection in such a way that **none can view His suffering in this film and walk away unchanged**.

A constitutional lawyer in Washington, DC. had this comment after seeing the film, ***The Passion of Christ***:

"...*The Passion*" evoked more **deep reflection, sorrow**

and emotional reaction within me than anything since my wedding, my ordination or the birth of my children. Frankly, **I will never be the same.**"

Of All Events in History—Only ONE EVENT Is Known as "*THE PASSION*"

The purpose of Christ's brutal suffering and death became abundantly clear: He did it all for love. He laid His life down for others, so that we can have peace with God. The laying down of one's life for someone else is the embodiment of PASSION. The PASSION of Christ was the ultimate expression of love. [3]

The lawyer, Keith Fournier, mentioned above, stated that no one can just "view" this film. It must be experienced. He stated that even in a crowd of seasoned politicians, there was not a dry eye in the house.

When personal sacrifice for another explodes into action, this is COMPASSION. Jesus showed compassion for you and me. No sacrifice can be greater than to give up your own life to benefit others. PASSION: willingness to suffer for the benefit of others.

Three Beatings—Three Opposing Groups

Jesus was mocked and fiercely beaten three times: first by Caiaphas and the other chief priests, then by Pilate's men, and finally by Herod's soldiers, that all might share in the guilt. Caiaphas was the chief priest, Pilot was the Roman governor, and Herod was the king of Judea at that time.

Pilot wrote with his own hand in Hebrew, Greek and Latin, utilizing the three main languages of the time, "Jesus of Nazareth, the King of the Jews."[4] This was so that all men could read the truth. Thus, all became responsible for the truth.

At the foot of the cross the rulers derided Him, the soldiers mocked Him, and even the criminals on the cross next to Him accused Him. Men, both great and small, rejected Him.[5]

Signs and wonders occurred at Jesus' death. The sun darkened for several hours at noonday followed by an earthquake. As He hung on the cross He asked God to forgive His enemies. Then He gave up His own life.[6]

The Word of God states that when a person comes into the kingdom of God they are grafted into the bloodline of Jesus. **(7) The plan of God to bring a redeemer for you and me could only be fulfilled with a perfect sacrifice. He gave His innocent life as a ransom and paid the ultimate price.(8) This sacrifice of the perfect Lamb of God was necessary, in order to offer salvation to you and me. Because we have all sinned, we all need a Savior.(9) He sacrificed His life that we might find eternal life, once again.(10)

Chapter Three
Beginnings

The passion of Christ is a simple, yet powerful love story that began in the Garden of Eden. There were two trees in the middle of the Garden, where the first man and woman lived, Adam and Eve. One was the tree of life and the other was the tree of the knowledge of good and evil. God forbid them from eating of the second tree and told them that if they did, they would die. However, the tree was very enticing and the fruit looked delicious.

One day, a serpent, who was Satan himself, seduced them into eating the forbidden fruit. He tempted them to **doubt the truth of God's Word**. When they disobeyed God, they gave up their position of rulership over the garden, and surrendered the right to eternal life. Satan became the legal ruler. Now mankind needed a Savior who was without sin, to redeem them and restore eternal life. That perfect Savior would have to "stand in" for all men and willingly die as a sacrifice. But because he had no sin, death could not legally hold Him. This enabled Him to rise from the dead, defeating death and restoring an opportunity for eternal life, once again.

Burning Bush

In the wilderness, Moses had an encounter with the Living God. God appeared to him in a burning bush and spoke His name to Moses: "*I Am*."

Jesus, as the Son of God, legally carried the name, I Am. On the night of His betrayal a mob came to arrest Him by force. He asked them whom they sought. They answered, "Jesus of Nazareth," He spoke the words, "*I Am*," and the armed men all fell to the ground, unable to move. Because Jesus was the "I Am," the sheer force of this statement caused strong men to faint. [11] No one took Him by force. He went willingly, for this was His destiny.

When Pilot interrogated Jesus, he asked if Jesus understood that he, Pilot, had the power to save Him or let Him go. Jesus answered that the only earthly power Pilot had over Jesus was allowed by God for a specific purpose. [12]

By an act of His own will, Jesus laid down His life. This selfless act of great PASSION gives us the opportunity to choose to believe that He is the Son of God, and that God raised Him from the dead. When we do not accept Jesus Christ as our Savior, it means rejecting the best friend we ever had, Who laid down His life for us.

Any clear thinking person would have to seriously consider a man's claim if he is willing to die for us, to give us a free gift. Consider accepting this invitation into the kingdom of God.

Chapter Four
A Picture of Total Love and Compassion

Significance of the Nails

The powerful striking sound of the nails Jesus received in His hands and feet signifies total commitment, no turning back for Yahshua the Messiah. There is no turning back for *us* once we are committed to walking free in Jesus. The horror of what Jesus endured brings us victory from demonic strongholds that come against our lives. The authority we are capable of walking in, is only limited by the amount of faith we are willing to exercise.

The nails used to impale Jesus to the cross were large spikes. As they pierced His hands and feet *(Psalm 22:16; John 20:25-29)* they were intended to help affect *our* deliverance all down through the ages. God, in His mercy, knew that all men needed great assistance in being set free and remaining free from the strongholds of the enemy. NAILS symbolize the Word of God, vows and unchangeable covenant promises. *...he fastened it with NAILS* **(vows or covenant promises)** *that it should not be moved. (Isaiah 41:7)*

The nails affixed Jesus' HANDS (which symbolize works, and guilt because of evil deeds) to the cross. **(13)** *Give them according to their deeds, and according to the wickedness of their HANDS... (Psalm 28:4)*

The guilt generated by evil deeds and weakness caused by shame, are the result of evil works. Nails affixed Jesus' FEET (which symbolize a person's walk) to the cross. **(14)** The *right side* represents natural things. The *left side* represents spiritual things. Jesus was pierced by a spear in the left side and blood ran out that cleanses us from our sin. The flow of His blood opened up a river of spiritual blessing that has never ceased, and His blood continually cleanses us from our sins. Most criminals were tied to the cross; the most *violent* offenders were nailed.

> *...the kingdom of heaven suffereth VIOLENCE, and the VIOLENT take it by FORCE. (Matthew 11:12)*

Jesus was the most VIOLENT offender to the kingdom of darkness Who ever lived. Jesus took the nails in His hands and feet, that our feet could be shod with the preparation of the gospel of peace. *(Ephesians 6:15)* He brought peace and goodwill toward men *(Luke 2:14)*, and a lively hope for redemption. *The kingdom of heaven is FORCEFULLY advancing and FORCEFUL men lay hold of it. (Matthew 11:12; Weymouth version)*

Palms Versus Wrists

Though some scientists have tried to invalidate the Word of God by declaring that Jesus was nailed through the wrists, claiming that the hand will not hold a man's weight, research supports the fact that it *is* possible to nail through the palm without breaking any bones and support considerable weight. There are several sites on the palm where this is possible, and each of these is capable of supporting a person's weight, without danger of tearing through the flesh, including the upper part of the palm, the ulnar (small finger) side of the wrist, and the radial (thumb) side of the wrist. The thenar furrow is located at the base of the thenar eminence muscles. These areas are capable of supporting hundreds of pounds. Research does support scripture, and debunks the notion that the wrists had to be used instead of the palms, at Jesus' crucifixion.[15]

Events Leading Up to Death

Jesus was in terrible mental anguish in the Garden of Gethsemane. His sweat became like (as) great drops of blood. He probably lost blood volume through profuse sweating and from sweating blood. There have been actual medically documented cases of people sweating blood under great duress.

Being scourged by the flagrum (or flagellum), a tool composed of strips of leather with pieces of metal and bone tied into it, exposed Jesus' nerve endings, muscles and skin, causing great trauma. As Jesus became exhausted, He would have experienced shivering, severe sweating, frequent seizures, hypovolemia (loss of fluid), and extreme thirst. Fluid would have begun to collect around His lungs from trauma. He was slapped and hit repeatedly. Thorns were placed on His head, assaulting the delicate nerve endings on His head. He probably entered a state of traumatic shock.[16]

While walking to Golgotha, water loss and shock would have worsened. When His hands were nailed to the cross with large, square iron nails, the probable damage to sensory branches known as the median nerve, would have caused one of the most extreme agonies known to man, exacerbated by the nailing of His feet. There had to have been excruciating agony every time Jesus moved, the hours on the cross with the weight of the body on the nails, unrelenting pain in the chest wall from the scourging, with the hot sun beating down. All this would have caused hypovolemic shock. If speculating from only a scientific standpoint, it is reasonable to conclude that Jesus died from shock, brought on by heart failure, caused by exhaustion, pain and loss of blood.[17]

However, there were greater factors than physical trauma affecting His death on the cross. Otherwise, He might have died after the scourging. Jesus had a powerful reason to survive the overwhelming physical torture until He, by an act of His own will, gave up His life at the appointed, preordained hour, as explained previously in the "*Amazing Passover*" section. He had to fulfill the types and shadows of the feast of Passover, completely. Our Savior accepted His role as a sacrificial lamb willingly, suffering unspeakable torture, pain and humiliation, to pay for the sins of billions of the sons of Adam, many of whom had not even been born yet.

When His heavenly Father released Him to do so, Jesus finally gave up His life, surrendering totally to His death. The PASSION was uniquely His to do, and His journey into hell was quickly followed by victory over death and hell when He rose again.

WHAT IS THE PASSION?

Three Crosses—Three Deaths

On opposite sides of the Messiah hung two thieves. They represented the sides or choices of fallen man. The first thief railed on Messiah, bitter and angry. He demanded a pardon without repentance. The second thief defended the Messiah, calling out to the other thief for the proper fear of God. Even in his hour of death, he asked to be saved. The third man on the cross, our Passover Lamb, hung between two thieves, sacrificing Himself to take away the sins of the world.

On Passover, there were three main sacrifices of lambs at the temple, rather than the usual two. The high priest always stood and did not sit until the last sacrifice. The **first** lamb was slain at the third hour, 9 AM *(Mark 15:24)*, the time when they nailed Jesus to the cross. The **second** sacrifice was at the sixth hour, 12 PM, when darkness covered the land, the time when the first thief spoke bitterly to Jesus. The temple sacrifice of the **third** lamb, the Passover lamb, was at the ninth hour, 3 PM, at the very moment Jesus died to take away the sins of the world. *(2 Corinthians 5:19)* After this final sacrifice, the high priest sat down in the temple mount, as our High Priest.

The first thief represented all who are deceived by the darkness of pride and unrepented sin, and died choosing to reject Messiah. The second thief chose the light, to follow Messiah even when things looked impossible. He represented all who turn back to Christ, even during trials or great offense. Jesus hung between the two—a choice for all mankind—for all time. He was a Savior willing to humble Himself even to the shame of the cross, to show us the way to truth, light and salvation.

Chapter Five
The Feasts of the LORD
Foreshadow Jesus

The feasts of the LORD, beginning with the Passover in Egypt, were given to the Hebrews to foreshadow Christ's coming. The spring feasts were fulfilled by His first coming and the fall feasts will be fulfilled when He returns.

The God of Abraham, Isaac and Jacob gave His people special Holy Days that are wonderful shadow pictures of things to come. The most revealing of the feasts foreshadowing the Messiah, was Passover.

Amazing Passover Feast Fulfilled

The shadow pictures in the Passover feast had been practiced by the Israelites every year since they left Egypt, yet they had no idea that Yahshua (Jesus) was the Messiah sent to fulfill every part of the feast. On the 10th of Aviv, Yahshua told His disciples to find Him a donkey's colt. Early that morning the high priest left the Temple Mount and went to the sheepfolds of Bethlehem where the sacrificial animals were bred. The path through the north gate was lined with priests standing shoulder to shoulder, holding palm fronds, just as they always had.

Once in Bethlehem, the high priest would select a perfect lamb and start back on the path toward the temple mount in Jerusalem, leading the lamb with a rope. The lamb would be inspected for four days to see if there was any defect in it.

On the appointed day to secure the Passover lamb, Yahshua (Jesus), *OUR* high priest, approached the city from the opposite direction, arriving before the other high priest. His disciples began shouting, *Blessed be the King that cometh in the Name of the LORD. (Luke 19:38)* Thousands of the Levites, not being able to see all the way up the path, began shouting this same phrase, as they had done for centuries. However, when they realized it was Yahshua, not the high priest they expected, they angrily ordered Him to hush His disciples. Jesus corrected them: *I tell you that, if these should hold their peace, the stones would immediately cry out. (Luke 19:40)*

At last, the true Passover Lamb, who was born in the sheep-folds of Bethlehem, entered the city where He was questioned and examined by the religious leaders for four days. Then His arrest and trial began, culminating with Pilot finishing the examination and sentencing Jesus. Pilot spoke the exact words that the high priest speaks when he has finished examining the Passover lamb, "I find no fault in Him."

At the moment of Jesus' arrest, when Peter tried to defend Him with a sword, Jesus spoke: *Put up thy sword into the sheath; the cup which My Father hath given Me, shall I not drink it? (John 18:11)* He was referring to the cup of suffering.

On the cross, when Yahshua knew His appointed hour was come, so that the scripture might be fulfilled, He cried out from the hill of Golgotha, *I thirst. (John 19:28)* Simultaneously, the high priest on the Temple Mount, just before killing the lamb, always said, "I thirst." After he drank from the cup set before him, he slit the throat of the lamb and caught the blood in a bowl, uttering the words, "It is finished." At that moment, Yahshua bowed His head and said, *It is finished. (John 19:30)* Immediately, an earthquake rent the rocks, ripping in two the many feet thick veil in the temple, symbolizing the destruction of the separation between God and man. The quake caused a crack in the ground next to the cross.

While, the high priest sprinkled the blood of the sacrificed lamb on the altar, the guard pierced Jesus' side and His blood flowed through the crack in the ground onto the mercy seat of the Ark of the Covenant, buried directly below over six-hundred years before, by Jeremiah. The perfect blood of Yahshua fulfilled the law once for all.[18] (Thanks to Michael Rood for some of the above Passover scenario.)

Sundown—Passover Begins

Traditionally, the Passover lamb was killed on the afternoon of the 14th day of Aviv, and put in the oven before sundown, and so Yahshua was killed and put in the grave before sundown, when Passover began.

At the first Passover in Egypt, blood was placed on the doorpost of every house, that death and judgment would pass them by. When we receive Jesus as our Passover Lamb, His blood is applied to the door of our hearts, that death will pass us by.

From the first Passover on, each house in Israel killed a Passover lamb, put the blood on their doors, and placed the lamb on a piece of wood in the shape of a cross with its entrails wrapped around it. Though they performed this ceremony for millennia, when the true Passover Lamb hung on a cross they did not recognize Him.

When the lamb was finished roasting, it was always to be consumed completely by every man, woman and child. They were miraculously made whole so that all walked out of Egypt, the land of idolatry and sin, perfectly healed, headed for God's promised land. We, too, are to utterly embrace all that our Savior accomplished for us as we walk by faith out of the land of death through His shed blood, completely healed, body, soul and spirit, by His finished work on the cross.

Upon death, Jesus' soul descended into hell to receive *our* rightful punishment upon Himself. But because He was without sin, death could not legally hold Him. Believing in Him as our Savior, and applying His blood to the doorposts of our hearts, means Satan has no legal right to hold us captive, either.

As Jesus rose from the grave on the third day, so the Israelites were to worship in the wilderness on the third day, being delivered from the bondage of death at the hand of the Egyptians. So, we too, are delivered from the wicked hand of Satan, because our Champion rose from the grave to give us eternal life.[19] As the cruel task masters, the Egyptians, were all destroyed in the waters

17

of the Red Sea, so our sins were washed away by our Messiah when He rose from the dead, victorious.[20]

Each of the seven feasts of the LORD carries great significance. Each foreshadows and rehearses what the Messiah would accomplish at His coming. First time as a suffering servant. Second time as a victorious king taking back His kingdom..

Spring Feasts:
> 1. Passover: Lamb sacrificed in Egypt. Lamb of God sacrificed for sin.
> 2. Unleavened Bread: Leaven represents sin. Messiah took away sin of world.
> 3. First Fruits: Harvest begins. Occurred day after Sabbath. Messiah rose from the dead this day.
> 4. Pentecost: After 40 days in wilderness, Hebrews experienced power of God as a mighty wind. 40 days after Jesus' resurrection the Holy Spirit came to the new church as a mighty wind.

Fall Feasts:
> 5. Feast of Trumpets: Celebrated by blowing trumpets. The last great trumpet will announce the gathering of His people.
> 6. Day of Atonement: A day of fasting and repentance. The judgment of the nations.
> 7. Feast of Tabernacles: Recalls Israel dwelling in wilderness in tents. Points to millennium when Messiah will come to dwell with men and be their King.

Chapter Six
The Shame of the Cross

The *shame* of the cross was worse than the *pain*. Paul calls the cross *"foolishness"* and a *"stumbling block."* *(1 Corinthians 1:18-25)* This is because the cross was used to humiliate. It was a public symbol of *indecency* and *obscenity*, intended to defame and crush a man's spirit. This is why crucifixion was always done in a public place. Golgotha was at a crossroads, just outside the city gates, where everyone passing could see. Roman law expressly forbid that a Roman citizen be crucified because of the extreme *stigma* and *offense* that the cross signified. In Greek romances, crucifixion was always circumvented in the end by the rescue of the hero. Pliny, the Younger, referred to Christianity as a "perverse and extravagant superstition," because it preached a crucified Messiah. A Savior who could be crucified was utter foolishness to the Greeks. The idea of a crucified Messiah was an oxymoron. In their minds the **Messiah bore the image of victory**, a conquering king, with power, but *not* the horror and shame associated with the cross.[21]

Peter, Jesus' disciple, spoke vehemently against Jesus when He revealed His upcoming crucifixion, and he was severely rebuked. Thomas, too, refused to believe after the resurrection. In the context of the stigma of the cross, it is not hard to understand why the disciples did not immediately believe on the morning of Jesus' resurrection, when women returned from the empty tomb excitedly announcing that He had risen.

Their failure to grasp this spiritual victory emanated from a culture replete with people who wished to take back their country from the Roman conquerors. The disciples were hiding together in a room, depressed and disappointed, their earthly hopes dashed, for they had hoped Jesus would arise and lead them to take the land by force. Clearly, they were looking for a Messiah who would come as a different kind of conquering hero, according to their culture's expectations.

This expectation is one of the reasons why Saul, a future apostle and a true legalist, was "breathing murderous threats," persecuting the early church to the death. *(Acts 22:4; 9:1)* The Jews insistence that Jesus be crucified was engineered to illicit the public's contempt and loathing for this Messiah. In Saul's view, YHWH, their God, had obviously cursed and rejected Yahshua as Messiah. The scriptures condemned anyone who was hung on a cross.

> *His body shall not remain all night upon the tree...For He that is hanged is accursed of God. (Deuteronomy 21:23)*

> *Cursed is everyone that hangeth on a tree. (Galatians 3:13)*

Calling Him the Messiah was outrageous blasphemy to Saul, who was a true legalist and understood the curse of the law. He was a Pharisee among Pharisees![22]

Chapter Seven
Archeology Supports Biblical Truths

Wrap your mind around this! An archeologist named Ron Wyatt began making a series of discoveries several years ago in the middle east. Among the many awe-inspiring things he found were Noah's ark in Turkey, the crossing place of the Hebrews at the Red Sea, and Sodom and Gomorrah.

Ron's most exciting discovery was the Ark of the Covenant buried directly under the hill known as Golgotha outside Jerusalem, where Jesus was crucified. For over 600 years the Ark of the Covenant had waited patiently for the momentous occasion of the Messiah's death.

When Jesus shouted His last maranatha cry from the cross, "*It is finished,*" and died, an earthquake caused a crack in the ground, knocking aside the top of the sarcophagus containing the legendary ark. This exposed the "mercy seat" where, for millennia before, the blood of a perfect lamb had been sprinkled once a year by the high priest of Israel, to atone for the sins of the people.

When the Roman guard speared Jesus' side, His blood, the blood of the perfect Lamb of God, ran down through the crack in the ground next to the cross created by the earthquake, directly onto the mercy seat of the ark of the covenant, fulfilling the law once for all. The "mercy seat" received the sinless blood of Jesus and the awesome plan of God was fulfilled.

When Ron Wyatt broke into the chamber containing the ark, he found blood spattered on the mercy seat of the ark, and on the walls. Taking samples of this blood, he had it tested by two independent laboratories. The same conclusion was reached by both. This blood was unique. It had 23 female chromosomes, and only one male chromosome. Normal blood has 23 of each. Ron concluded that this was the matchless blood of Jesus Christ Whose mother was Mary, and Whose father was God, Himself.

At the top of the chamber containing the ark, Ron found cracks in the ground. Upon investigating the top of the hill, he found a corresponding crack in the earth next to a deliberate indentation in the ground. He believed this was the very spot that held upright the cross of Calvary.[23]

Recently, archeologists have discovered a series of secret tunnels under the temple mount that could have been used to secret away the ark to a safe place. It is believed that Jeremiah, the prophet, hid the ark during the Babylonian invasion.

Chapter Eight
Who Is Guilty for Jesus' Death?

The story of Jesus' death is a deeply moving, profoundly human story. It touches us on a level that no other story ever has. Jesus, Himself, was a Jew, but He died, not just for the Jews, but for all mankind.

Jesus was an innocent man, the perfect Lamb of God. The Bible states that the princes and rulers would not have crucified Him if they had understood who He was, and what would be accomplished by His death.[24]

At the moment Jesus was arrested, Peter, one of His closest disciples who was given to fits of passion, cut off a man's ear with his sword. Even at that moment, Jesus' compassion arose. He healed the man's ear and told Peter that it was God's will for Him to be arrested. Jesus was denied three times by Peter. However, when Peter repented and was converted, he became a leader in the newly established church.

Jesus was betrayed for thirty pieces of silver by Judas, one of His twelve disciples. The treacherous Judas led a multitude with torches and swords to make the arrest, and he identified Jesus by giving Him a kiss on the cheek.

Jesus was persecuted to the death by several different groups: the religious crowd, the political crowd, the throngs gathered in Jerusalem for the Passover feast, and the king of Judah. This is an amazingly broad spectrum of opposition. Representatives from every segment of society participated in bringing Him to the cross.

At the time of Jesus' death, it was Passover season. Each year a perfect lamb was sacrificed for the whole nation of Israel.

Who Is to Blame?

Who can we blame for Jesus' death? The Jews, the king, the priests, the Romans, the common people, Judas?

Can we point a finger at the Jews? No! Jesus clearly stated that He gave His own life as a ransom for many.

Can we blame the chief priests? No, it was part of the plan that they would not recognize the Messiah. As representatives for the whole nation, they should have known the scriptures. Instead, they were fearful that Jesus would start a revolution and destroy their positions with the Roman government, fomenting Roman retribution against them. They were protecting their jobs and their way of life, as the guardians of traditions handed down for more than a thousand years.

Can we blame the king? Actually, Herod had long desired to meet Jesus, that he might witness some miracle at Jesus' hands. He had no desire for Jesus' death. Additionally, political maneuvering dictated that he defer to Pilot. He and Pilot became allies after Jesus' death.

Can we blame the Romans? No, because He laid down His own life by His own free will. The Romans played a part in the plan of God from Jesus' birth. By decree of Caesar Augustus, Mary and Joseph were compelled to go to Bethlehem to register for taxes. On this mandatory journey, Jesus was born in a lowly stable and laid in a manger.

Can we blame the common people of that time? No more than any other man. Tens of thousands had come to Jerusalem for a festival, and they were caught in the heat of the moment, the roar of the crowd. Have you ever experienced a frenzied mob? Think of all the people trampled to death at soccer games and rock concerts.

Can we blame Judas? Judas was the disciple who handled all the money. In modern day society, almost every day the news carries the story of someone who handles large amounts of money taken over by greed. Wall Street scandals and corporate avarice abound. Jesus knew who Judas really was, yet at the Last Supper He told Judas to go quickly to do what he must do. It was part of the plan. Judas betrayed Jesus for only thirty pieces of silver.

Can you and I take the blame? Because of the fall of all mankind and our collective sin, we *all* fall short of perfection. It is our sins that put Jesus on the cross, and His love that kept Him there.

Seeing the movie, *The Passion of Christ*, in Washington, DC. moved another law professor to tell his friend, "After watching this film, I do not understand how anyone can insinuate that it even remotely presents that the Jews killed Jesus. It doesn't. IT MADE ME REALIZE THAT MY SINS KILLED JESUS!"

Anyone who distorts the reason for Jesus' death quite simply has another agenda. Perhaps a dictator needs a scapegoat to blame for societies' troubles, to consolidate their own power base as Hitler did. Perhaps villainization of certain people groups is utilized to exalt another religion.

Remember, the very same people who waved palm branches welcoming Jesus into Jerusalem four days earlier, turned on Him at His trial, screaming "Crucify Him" at Pilot's judgment seat. He willingly became the Passover Lamb that takes away the sins of the world, slain for you and me. His death and resurrection was a door to everlasting life. for all mankind, that *all men* might have access to the kingdom of God.

In the next two sections of this book, we will take a detailed look at the specific aspects of the torture of Jesus, and what their significance is to us. Each part of His suffering had meaning and purpose. Each time His blood flowed, it opened the door of salvation wider for us. The thorns, and the beatings, the mocking and the shame are examined. The spitting and plucking, scourging and nailing are examined. God has revealed each part of His suffering to me and what benefits were achieved by each event. The most incredible part is the revelation of His blood and what it means in our daily lives. Please understand that what God has revealed is more than anyone can comprehend fully, but even to revel in His wisdom for a moment brings such joy and excitement that to live without acknowledging His love is inconceivable. God so loved His creation, that He gave His only begotten Son, to be tortured, with great shame and death, so that His shed blood could pay the price for man's sin, past present and future.

God's own blood flowed in His Son's veins, just as every Father's blood flows in His son's and daughter's veins. Just as the life of a man is in the blood, God's life is in Jesus' blood. When Jesus' blood was spilled, His life was released into the world to accomplish the grand purpose God had intended from the beginning. Jesus was obedient and that's all we need to be. Praise Him for His perfection and His obedience and for His willingness to suffer for us—His PASSION!

There are two more books in this series. The next is about the *Stripes* He bore for us. The Stripes are for our healing, and revelation of this portion of Jesus' PASSION is so extensive as to require a book all its own. The third part is what I call Advanced Christianity. The application of spiritual warfare, as revealed to me through the Holy Spirit, represented by the *Nails* that fastened Jesus to the cross. Also, extensive and quite detailed.

The next two books to be published in this series are about the *Stripes* and the *Nails* and their powerful significance for our lives.

Bibliography for Part One

1. *Greater love hath no man than this, that a man lay down his life for his friends. (John 15:13)*
2. *Strong's Exhaustive Concordance* 3958, pascho
3. Acts 1:3
4. John 19:19
5. Luke 23:35-39
6. *...give His life a ransom for many. (Mark 10:45)*
7. *For if the firstfruit be holy, the lump is also holy: and if the root (Jesus) be holy, so are the branches (Jews). And if some of the branches be broken off, and thou, being a wild olive tree (gentile believers), wert grafted in among them, and with them partakest of the root and fatness of the olive tree; Boast no against the branches (Jews)... (Romans 11:16-18)*
8. *...I lay down My life, that I might take it again. No man taketh it from me, but I lay it down of Myself... (John 10:17-18)*
9. *For all have sinned, and come short of the glory of God. (Romans 3:23)*
10. *To whom He showed Himself alive after His PASSION by many infallible proofs, being seen of them forty days, and speaking of the things pertaining to the kingdom of God. (Acts 1:3)*
11. *Jesus therefore, knowing all things that should come upon Him, went forth, and said unto them, Whom seek ye? They answered Him, Jesus of Nazareth. Jesus saith unto them, I am He. And Judas also, which betrayed Him, stood with them. As soon then as He had said, unto them, I am He, they went backward, and fell to the ground. (John 8:4-6)*
12. Jesus answered, Thou couldest have no power at all against Me, except it were given thee from above... (John 19:11)
13. Milligan, *Understanding The Dreams You Dream*, Treasure House 1993, p. 16118
14. Ibid. p. 146-146
15. Zugibe, "*Two Questions About Crucifixion*," Bible Review, April, 1989, pp. 35-42
16. Primrose, "*A Surgeon Looks At Crucifixion*," Hibbert Journal, 47, 1949, pp. 382-388
17. Zubige, Ibid. pp. 40-41
18. Portions of Passover scenario taken from the teachings of Rabbi Michael Rood
19. *And having spoiled principalities and powers, He made a show of them openly, triumphing over them in it. (Colossians 2:15)*
20. *Who hath delivered us from the power of darkness, and hath translated us into the kingdom of His dear Son. (Colossians 1:13)*
21. Storms, "Jesus, *the Suffering Savior: The Obscenity of the Cross*," pp. 3-4 (Personal thanks to Dr. Sam Storms for assistance in gathering info. on the crucifixion)
22. Ibid. p. 45
23. Wyatt, *Discovered Volume*, pp.95-101
24. *Which none of the princes of this world knew: for had they known it, they would not have crucified the LORD of glory. (I Corinthians 2:8)*

Part Two

THORNS

The crown of thorns
precedes the crown of glory

Thorns

from the *Heart & Soul Surrender* CD
Lyrics by Bree Keyton

The crown of thorns *(Mark 15:17)* that Jesus wore was an attack on the soulish realm; mind, will, emotions, imagination and memory, where the *real* battles take place. Thorns represent the hindrances, evil circumstances, and cares of this life. *(Matthew 13:22)* He could never lean His head to rest from the unrelenting pain as the thorns bit into His flesh. He suffered this to provide us rest from the ceaseless attacks of Satan against our souls *(1 Peter 4:12)*, through leaning on Christ and His protection against the fiery darts of the wicked one. *(Ephesians 6:16)*

Thorns and thistles were part of the curse, and a sign of our sin. *(Genesis 3:11-18)* But He Who knew no sin became sin for us, that we might have eternal life. *(2 Corinthians 5:21)* He bore the curse on His own head, that we might have the mind of Christ. *(1 Corinthians 2:16)* Blood from the thorn's wounds fell on the ground to cleanse it and deliver us from the curse.

The first Adam was condemned to labor among the thorns and thistles to bring forth a harvest. *(Genesis 3:17)* The last Adam wore the thorns and a robe of purple *(John 19:2)* that stood for purple thistles, to bring forth a harvest of souls. *(Mark 15:17)* Jesus gave us the weapons of our warfare. They are *not* carnal, but mighty through God to the pulling down of strongholds, casting down imaginations, and every high thing that exalts itself against the knowledge of God, bringing into captivity every thought to the obedience of Christ. *(2 Corinthians 10:4-5; Ephesians 6)*

His thorns became our helmet of salvation. *(Ephesians 6:17)*

The crown of thorns precedes the crown of glory. *(1 Peter 5:4)*

Chapter Nine
Thorns: A Metaphor for Sin

Thorns illustrate and symbolize sin: Under the beauty of the rose, lurks the pain and ugliness of a thorn. As thorns pierce in (Jesus' side was pierced), they draw blood (He shed His blood for us), they make holes (holes left in Jesus' hands and feet), and can shred flesh (the scourging shredded His flesh): Thorns became a metaphor for sin and punishment. As we meditate on what Jesus endured for us, our love blooms and flourishes. Jesus is the "Lily" and "the Rose" *(Song of Solomon 2:1)*, Who took the thorns for us on His head, and set us free from the damaged or wounded memories that Satan uses to torment us. He bore the curse in His own body. *(Galatians 3:13)*

The Curse of the Thorns and Thistles

As our Savior wore the *"crown of thorns,"* it was a constant, painful reminder that He bore for us the chastisement for our peaceful reconciliation with the Father. The Roman soldiers intended to mock Him by imitating the crown of laurel leaves and purple robe that Caesar wore in his claim to deity, whenever he returned to Rome victorious. However, when Jesus wore the crown of thorns and the purple robe, it represented the thorns and purple thistles of the curse that came on all mankind in the Garden of Eden. He transformed these things into noble symbols even in His humiliation, as He bore our sins and carried our sorrows. He alone could perform this astounding feat, for only He, among all men who have ever lived, was *truly* deity. Following is the Word spoken to Adam in the Garden by God after he sinned.

> *...cursed is the ground for thy sake; in sorrow shalt thou eat of it all the days of thy life; THORNS ALSO AND THISTLES shall it bring forth to thee... (Genesis 3:17-18)*

The curse, that after the perfection of Eden we should toil on ground that brings forth thorns and thistles, was unwittingly fulfilled through the soldiers' cruelty. Thorns tear the flesh, as His flesh was torn for us. Jesus became a curse for us, and restored the blessings and favor of God.

Thorns: The Place of the Skull

Jesus was crucified at Golgotha, which means place of the skull. This was no accident. The skull is where we must be crucified daily, allowing God to mold us into His image. Because of the fall, there is a curse against our minds. Jesus redeemed our minds, so that now we can receive the mind of Christ. *(1 Corinthians 2:16)* Messiah's mind is not our mind until He fully owns us, and we can not become fully His until we surrender to His plan for our lives.

Part of Jesus' PASSION was to wear the helmet of salvation, known as the "*crown of thorns*," but He won for *us* the helmet of salvation *(Ephesians 6:17)* to war against the enemy, a weapon *proven in battle* through His victorious resurrection, to protect our minds from the constant bombardment of our thought lives. As we allow ourselves to be conformed to Christ's image through renewing our *minds*, we wear this helmet, trusting in the perfectly fitted armor He molded for us in His image, for we know the One Who *proved* it. He demonstrated to us that it works. **Then came Jesus forth, wearing the CROWN OF THORNS... (John 19:5)**

Pulling Down Strongholds

How is it possible to pull down strongholds in our minds? Because Jesus was tempted just as we are, yet without sin. *(Hebrews 4:15)* The evil desires of our carnal flesh *can* be harnessed. How? Because the weapons Jesus gave us are *not* carnal. They have been tried in severe fires of affliction, so extreme that you and I can only imagine them. He wore the *"crown of thorns"* on His head so that we would be able, through Him, to pull down strongholds, the desires of carnal flesh that exalt themselves against the knowledge of God. *(1 Corinthians 10:4-5)* His thorns become our helmet of salvation. *(Ephesians 6)* Some day we will wear a crown of glory with Him in His kingdom. *(1 Peter 5:4)*

Sin Personified

Sin is personified in the Bible beginning in Genesis 4:7. It is personally lying in wait for you. You have a choice to open the DOOR and let it into your heart, or keep it closed each and every day. Sin may enter through wiles, the trickery of the devil, gaining a legal foothold in your heart to torment and confuse you. It will steal your peace, rob your joy, drag in guilt and shame, and introduce you to ever deeper realms of wickedness.

> *...if thou doest not well, sin LIETH at the DOOR. And unto thee shall be HIS DESIRE, and thou shalt rule over him.*

The word LIETH (*Strong's* 7257, rabats) means to crouch or hide on all four legs like a recumbent animal. This is a vivid picture of how the devil lies in wait to pounce on us as we open the portal to sin through our own acts of disobedience. *The Amplified Bible* is illuminating on this scripture.

> *...if you do not do well, SIN CROUCHES AT YOUR DOOR; its desire is for you, and you must master it. (Genesis 4:7)*

Sin was crouching at Cain's door, the first son of Adam and Eve after the fall, just as it is crouching at our doors. Cain failed the temptation and reacted in rage. He displeased almighty God, failing to offer a blood sacrifice (early foreshadowing of Jesus' death). Instead, he offered grain as a sacrifice. His brother, Abel, offered an animal sacrifice, and God was pleased with him. Enraged, jealousy and revenge overtook Cain. He murdered his brother.

Jesus Conquered Sin

Jesus mastered sin by successfully resisting the temptation

to kill His enemies. Instead, He forgave them. Thereby He defeated Satan on the cross, that we, too, could master sin in Jesus' Name, take up *our* crosses and follow Christ.

Jesus stands at the door of our hearts. He will not deceive us to gain entry, or launch stealth attacks to defeat our wills. He knocks. We can open the door and He will come in and dwell in our hearts in mercy and love. He will bring wisdom, peace and joy as free gifts. ***Behold, I*** (Jesus) ***stand at the DOOR, and knock: if any man hear My voice, and open the door, I will come in to him, and will sup with him, and he with Me. (Revelation 3:20)***

Chapter Ten
Attacks Against the Mind

The Mind is Focal Point of Attack

The mind, being the focal point of Satan's attack on us, becomes high ground in the battle against Satan. When ancient pagan peoples worshipped their gods, they worshipped on high ground, called high places or groves. Among Satan's arsenal of weapons is his ability to attack our high places (our minds). Satan is a constant aggressor and bombards us daily, sometimes hundreds of times a day, though we are not always aware of it, with thoughts of unclean origin. Among *our* arsenal of weapons is the spoken Word of God, the blood of Jesus which covers us, the Name of Jesus which He gave us to use, and unwavering faith, without which it is impossible to please God.

To overcome the human tendency to give in to temptation, Jesus fasted and was tempted in the wilderness for forty days at the beginning of His ministry. He proved that even in our weakness, we are made strong through our God.

The physical body begins to die after forty days without food. Satan came to Jesus in His physical weakness to tempt Him to turn the stones into bread to satisfy His hunger, offering Him worldly power, and further tempting Him to react with pride. Yet, Jesus defeated His enemy in this battle. Satan will tempt you in your moments of weakness in all the same ways, through lusts of the flesh, lusts of the eyes and the pride of life.

The Connection Between Heart and Mind

In recent months, a Japanese doctor has made a discovery revealing that there are brain cells in the heart. Scientists have long sought to make the connection between the heart and the mind, which is undeniable. The Bible made this connection thousands of years ago in scriptures such as: *for as he THINKETH IN HIS HEART, so is he… (Proverbs 23:7)* and *…for out of the abundance of the HEART the MOUTH SPEAKETH. (Matthew 12:34)*

In the book, *Heart and Mind are Intertwined*, by Daniel DeNoon, the connection of mental health with heart health is explored. The mind, according to DeNoon, affects the immune system, and the immune system affects the heart. Anger increases the risk of heart attack two-fold, while mental stress causes obstruction of the arteries in 30 to 60% of cases with coronary artery disease. Even depression and hostile personalities take a toll on the heart and immune function. The effects are cumulative.

In the grip of violent emotions such as fear, the heart will react, sometimes producing a heart attack. After our nation was assaulted on 9-11, hospitals filled up with people suffering from heart troubles. Fear gripped our nation.

Psychological Warfare

Thoughts shot into our minds from Satan's arsenal are most accurately defined as propaganda. They are just like the propaganda of modern warfare. The goal is to demoralize victims by any method possible.

Lies and half-truths are propagated, and if you receive these lies, then the battle for your homeland (your mind) is lost. Demons are often assigned to speak the same lie in a person's mind several times a day for a whole lifetime. To win this battle, it is necessary to launch a resistance that is equally persistent.

During the recent Gulf War, our own troops dropped thousands of leaflets in enemy territory saying things like, "It is futile to resist. Drop your weapons and join our side." They played heavy metal music at high volumes that terrified the Iraqis.

A prophet of God from Romania, Dumitru Dudaman, was shown a vision of the devil's tactics. In his vision, Satan stood in front of a group of Christians and challenged them: "Who wants to fight?" When 25% indicated they did, he told them to stand apart from the rest. Then he turned and killed the other 75% **who did not wish to fight**.

Personal Attacks

Other tactical warfare methods used by Satan's army are personal attacks against you to demoralize or take the wind out of your sails, through shame and guilt over past sins. Even if you have repented of the sins, Satan is frequently successful at reminding you of your unworthiness and causing you to hang your head and agree that all is lost, hope is gone. The result is a warrior with his defenses down, vulnerable to the next round of attack.

When this happens, simply remind the devil that *you*, unlike him, are forgiven, and that when *you* repent, your sins are obliterated by the blood of your Savior. Tell him that after all, it is not about your own righteousness anyway, but the righteousness of your Savior Who cleanses you from sin. Satan's eternal destiny, on the other hand, is permanently sealed with no chance of pardon, in the lake of fire.

> *And the devil that DECEIVED them was cast into the lake of fire and brimstone…and shall be tormented day and night for ever and ever. (Revelation 20:10)*

Mixing Truth with Lies

Other offensive incursions into the minds of humans involve mixing the truth with lies to bring confusion. Con artists, thieves and opportunists of all kinds have employed this tactic for personal gain for thousands of years, ever since Adam and Eve's expulsion from the garden. The father of lies became our father the moment the first Adam yielded to temptation and sin. If one lie of the enemy is accepted into your mind, others will follow. It is even better for demons if they can coerce their victims into speaking lies out of their own mouths, such as judgments against others, rumors, false blame, bitter words.

Negativity attracts demons because it can be used as a wedge to divide and conquer. Negativity engenders bitterness, offense, hatred, blame, and feeds hurts and wounds. Demons of the same name can easily attach themselves to each negative sinful emotion and make it worse. All praise to our Messiah for coming to deliver us from the deceiver. Satan's only weapon now is *deception*. He goes about *as* a roaring lion, seeking whom he may devour. Reconnaissance against these tactics and effectual homeland defense requires vigilant:

1. Daily repentance and prayer.
2. Fervent intercession.
3. Strategic spiritual warfare.

Using these methods we ask for a Holy Spirit lockdown on demonic activity. Remember that through sin we open ourselves up to Satan's legal authority to harassment and possible defeat on numerous fronts. Staying in a constant state of humble repentance, always remembering "Whose" you are, will strengthen you.

Pride Crucified at Place of the Skull

Thorns remind us, through pain, not to allow ourselves to be puffed up. Pride is a killer. The Apostle Paul's "thorn" in the flesh (*Strong's* 4647, skolops), means withered at the front, bodily annoyance or disability. The word comes from skelos (4628) meaning the leg, leanness, to parch. This attack against Paul by a demonic force was divinely permitted satanic antagonism.

> ***And lest I should be exalted above measure through the abundance of the revelations, there was given to me a THORN in the flesh, the messenger of Satan to BUFFET me, lest I should be exalted above measure. (2 Corinthians 12:7-8)***

The BUFFETING of Paul was probably painful, humiliating, and caused great suffering. BUFFET means a recurrent action. When we are willing to humble ourselves under the mighty hand of the living God, and refuse to think more highly of ourselves than we should, then God does not have to humble us. We allow our ourselves to be nailed to the cross daily, with Christ.

Thorns symbolize lowliness of the mind, humility. The King of Glory laid aside His heavenly crown and grandeur to be born in a lowly stable, and to die in shame. He came to earth meek and lowly to show us a better way. In our weakness, we desire to exalt ourselves, and legislate the King of Kings out of our earthly affairs. The arrogance of men puffs itself up above a holy God. Benjamin Franklin made the following statement at the Constitutional Convention.

> "In the beginning of the contest with Great Britain, when we were sensible of danger, we had daily prayers in this room for divine protection. Our prayers, sir, were heard and they were graciously answered. All of us, endangered in the struggle, must have observed **frequent instances of a superintending Providence** in our favor. And have we now **forgotten that powerful Friend**? Or do we imagine that we no longer need His assistance? I have lived, sir, a long time, and the longer I live, the more convincing proofs I see of this truth—that **God governs in the affairs of men**."

We must always remember that the hand of Jesus, stretched forth to extend mercy to all mankind, is a nail-scarred hand. A price was paid for us that can never be revoked.

Spiritual Warfare

The devil remains a powerful force to deal with for those who are not born again, and those who do not believe in or employ spiritual warfare. (Much more on this subject in the *Nails* book.) Jesus' nails, thorns, stripes, His blood and His death were endured for our sakes to set us free. Do not delay in receiving Jesus Christ as your Savior today. The attacks against your thoughts are Satan's bullets, an enemy tactic to demoralize and destroy you. Evil thoughts will come, but this is not sin. It only *becomes* sin when you *take* the thoughts, and let them have a place in your heart.

Turning an evil thought over and over in your mind is a sign that spiritual warfare needs to take place against that thought and take authority over the demon who originated it. Demons love to attach themselves to a person's evil thoughts and stir and energize them.

Put on the helmet of salvation right now! Cleanse your thought life. Resist the enemy; defeat him *before* he gains a foothold in your thought life. Apply the blood of Jesus to your mind daily, and bind scriptures to yourself for protection, deliverance and healing. Resist wicked thoughts; claim the victory before you see it, in Jesus' Name.

Prayer for Salvation

Jesus (Yahshua) I am a sinner, but I repent of all my sins right now in the Name of Jesus, the Christ of Nazareth (Yahshua the Messiah). Please forgive me and wash me clean in the blood of the perfect Lamb Who died for me. Jesus, I believe You are the Son of God (YHWH) and that He raised You from the dead. I speak these words with my mouth and I believe them in my heart.

If thou shalt confess with thy mouth the LORD Jesus, and shalt believe in thine heart that God hath raised Him from the dead, thou shalt be saved. For with the heart man believeth unto righteousness; and with the mouth confession is made unto salvation.

(Romans 10:9) Now, by faith, I believe I am born again. I receive eternal life through my Savior, Jesus Christ. Thank you, Jesus, for saving me. Amen.

Part Three

THE BLOOD

*We are overcomers through
the blood of the Lamb*

The Blood

from the *Heart & Soul Surrender* CD
Lyrics by Bree Keyton

We are overcomers through the shed blood of the Lamb *(Revelation 12:11)*, **and it's power to save, protect, redeem and continuously cleanse us.** *(Revelation 7:14)* **The first Adam had his side opened in a deep sleep and a bride was taken out.** *(Revelation 2:21-22)* **The last Adam's side was pierced while in the deep sleep of death, and a bride was taken out, created through His blood.** *(John 19:34)*

Jesus sweat as great drops of blood at Gethsemane *(Luke 22:44)*, **to set us free from rebellion, fear, and stubbornness, that in our moments of weakness, we are made strong.** *(2 Corinthians 12:9; 13:4)* **He took blows to His face, received stripes, wore the crown of thorns, His hands and feet nailed to the cross, His side pierced, until blood streamed from every part of His body, to make us free from head to foot.** *(John 18:22; Matthew 26:67; Mark 15:17-19; John 19:34; John 20:25)*

God spared not His own Son *(Romans 8:32)* **that He may freely give us all things. Jesus was punished that we might be forgiven.** *(Colossians 1:14)*

He took the cup of suffering *(John 18:11)*, **that we might drink from the well of living water.** *(John 4:10)*

He was betrayed for thirty pieces of silver *(Matthew 26:15; Zechariah 11:12)*, **that we might receive the priceless riches of His free grace.** *(1 Peter 3:7)*

He was betrayed by the kiss of a friend *(Mark 14:10; Psalm 49:1)*, **that He could be our friend, Who sticks closer than a brother.** *(Proverbs 8:24)*

Jesus was sorrowful and very heavy *(Matthew 26:38)*, **suffering emo-**

tionally to the point of death *(Luke 22:43)*, that we could wear the garment of praise *(Isaiah 61:3)* in all life's circumstances.

There were false witnesses *(Matthew 26:60-61)*, that we might have an advocate, Who ever makes intercession for us. *(Hebrews 7:25)*

He was hated without a cause *(John 15:23-25; Psalm 69:4)*, that we could be loved as sons. *(1 John 3:2)*

He spoke truth that sealed His death *(Mark 14:62)*, that we might speak the truth of eternal life. *(1 John 5:13)*

He was abused and mocked by the chief priests, by Herod's men, and by Pilot's men, that we might all know the need for a Savior. *(Matthew 26:67-68; 27:28; Mark 14:65; Luke 23:10-11)*

He wore scarlet to bear the scarlet sins of the world. *(2 Corinthians 5:19)*

He was blindfolded that we might see *(Mark 14:65; Luke 22:64)*, and bound to set us free. *(John 8:36)*

Guards smote Him on the head with a reed *(Mark 15:19)*, that we might be conformed to the image of Christ. *(Romans 8:29)*

They spit on Him *(Isaiah 50:6)*, heaping on rejection *(Isaiah 50:3)*, that we could be accepted in the beloved. *(Ephesians 1:6)*

They plucked out His beard *(Isaiah 50:6)*, humbling Him, that we might be exalted. *(James 1:9)*

They reviled Him *(Psalm 109:25)* and set Him at naught *(Luke 23:11)*, that we might be seated in heavenly places. *(Ephesians 2:6)*

He was vehemently accused *(Luke 23:10)*, that we might be justified by grace, through faith. *(Romans 3:24-25)*

He was delivered for envy *(Mark 15:10)*, that all things may work together for good to them that love God. *(Romans 8:28)*

THE BLOOD

He received blows to His face *(Mark 14:65)*, that our wounded hearts may be healed. They smote Him with their hands *(John 18:22; 19:3; Matthew 26:67)*, that we might turn the other cheek. *(Matthew 5:39)*

He was dumb before His shearers *(Isaiah 53:7; Matthew 26:62-63)*, that we might have an answer for every accusation. *(Luke 12:11-12; Matthew 27:37; 1 Peter 3:15)*

He was stripped *(Matthew 27:28)*, that we might be clothed with humility. *(1 Peter 5:5)*

The first Adam stripped us naked through rebellion *(Genesis 2:17)*, shamed when he knew he was naked. *(Genesis 3:10)* The last Adam suffered shame in public nakedness *(Hebrews 13:12-13)*, and by obedience to the cross, clothed us in robes of righteousness. *(Isaiah 61:10)*

By the offense of one, judgment came on all; by the righteousness of the other, eternal life came to all who receive it. *(Romans 5:18)*

His visage was so marred, He didn't even look human *(Isaiah 52:14)*, that one day we might behold His matchless beauty. *(Revelation 1:13-18)*

He was condemned and punished *(Mark 14:64; Matthew 26:66; Isaiah 53:3-5)*, so that God could be for us and none could stand against us. *(Romans 8:31)*

He gave His back to the smiters *(Isaiah 50:3; Matthew 26:67)*, to break off our rebellion. *(Proverbs 17:11)*

He bore the cross *(John 19:17)*, that we can roll our cares on Him. *(1 Peter 5:7)*

He stumbled and fell, that we might receive strength for every trial. *(Hebrews 12:10)*

Another man picked up His cross *(John 12:32)*, that we might pick up our crosses and follow Christ. *(Matthew 16:24)*

He was crucified in disgrace outside the city *(Hebrews 13:11-13)*, where all that passed at the crossroads set eyes on Him, that we may enter into the presence of our heavenly Father without shame, and preach the gospel to all who stand at the crossroads of life.

He was lifted up on the cross, as the serpent was in the wilderness *(Numbers 21:9)*, that all who look to Him for healing may also find salvation, and that He could draw all men to Him, bearing our wickedness and bringing healing to our souls and bodies. *(John 12:32)*

He bore our sins in His own body on the tree *(1 Peter 2:24)*, that we could be trees of righteousness. *(Isaiah 61:2)*

He was crucified in weakness *(1 Corinthians 13:4)*, but we shall live with Him forever by the power of God. *(2 Corinthians 13:4)*

He became a curse, that we might receive the blessing. *(Galatians 3:13-14)*

He was despised *(Isaiah 53:3)*, that we might receive honor *(2 Timothy 2:21)*, and rejected *(Isaiah 53:3)* that we might have acceptance. *(Ephesians 1:6)*

He was oppressed *(Isaiah 53:7)* and derided *(Luke 23:35)*, that we might be conformed into His image. *(Romans 8:29)*

He was acquainted with grief *(Isaiah 53:3)*, that we might rejoice in our salvation. *(1 Peter 1:8)*

He carried our sorrows, yet we esteemed Him stricken, smitten of God and afflicted. He was wounded for our transgressions, He was bruised for our iniquities, the chastisement of our peace was upon Him, and with His stripes we are healed. *(Isaiah 53:3-5; 1 Peter 2:24)*

Jesus took all of this in order to satisfy the great and wonderful and intense love with which He loved us, that God might clearly demonstrate through the ages to come, the immeasurable, limitless, surpassing riches of His free grace and unmerited favor, in kindness of heart toward us. *(Ephesians 2:4-7)*

They offered Him vinegar mixed with gall *(Matthew 27:34)*, but He refused to take the bitterness, that we might walk in love *(Ephesians 5:2)*, and that He might experience the full extent of suffering for us. *(Mark 9:12)*

They parted and ripped the garments worn closest to His flesh *(Psalm 22:18)*; just as the veil was rent in twain in the Holy of Holies *(Matthew 27:51)* that symbolized His body, to open a way for us to God. *(Hebrews 9:28)* They cast lots for His outer vesture, which was left whole *(John 19:24)*, for it was a valuable and seamless garment, as our new relationship with God through Christ is a valuable and seamless garment.

He forgave them *(Luke 23:34)*, and it was a vital part of the release of the power of the Holy Spirit into the earth, enabling Him to be raised from the dead *(Colossians 1:18; Acts 2:24)*, that we too, through forgiveness, can be raised up to sit together in heavenly places with Him. *(Ephesians 2:6)*

He thirsted and took plain vinegar *(John 19:28-30)*, that we might hunger and thirst after righteousness *(Matthew 5:6)*, drink of Christ, and be filled.

They railed on Him *(Mark 15:29)*, that we may glory in our weakness. *(2 Corinthians 12:9)*

He hung in darkness *(Luke 23:44)*, that we might walk in the light. *(1 John 1:7)*

He was forsaken by God *(Matthew 27:46)*, so that God would never leave or forsake us. *(Hebrews 3:5)*

He took God's wrath *(1 Thessalonians 1:10)*, that we might know God's mercy. *(Ephesians 2:4-7)*

He cried with a loud voice, "It is finished!" *(John 19:30)* The old covenant was fulfilled, and through it we received salvation. *(John 3:16)*

In death, He commended His spirit into His Father's hands *(Luke 23:46)*, that we may die to self *(1 Corinthians 15:31)*, and yield our will, trusting all in the Father's hands.

God's earthquake released such power that death lost its grip on many captives. *(Matthew 27:51)*

No bones were broken *(John 19:36)*, for He gave His body as a bridge between God and man.

Jesus tasted death for every man, that we might have life everlasting. *(1 Timothy 1:16)* Through His death He destroyed him who had the power over death *(Luke 23:46; John 19:30)*, the devil *(Hebrews 2:14)*, and He led captivity captive. *(Ephesians 4:8)* He died our death, that we might share His life.

Spices and myrrh were used for His burial. *(John 19:14)* The vessel that was His body was broken *(1 Corinthians 11:24)*, that the precious ointment, His blood, could pour forth as a sweet fragrance on all flesh, for His love is as ointment poured forth. *(Song of Solomon 1:3)*

Though He was bound in grave clothes *(Matthew 27:59)*, He cast them off and rose from the grave a victorious champion *(1 Corinthians 15:54-57)*, that we, too, could be unchained, and cast off the grave clothes and arise to life in Him. *(Hebrews 10:9)*

An angel's voice trumpeted the good news that He is risen *(Matthew 28:6)*, for Jesus Christ conquered hell and death *(Psalm 16:10; Revelation 20:13-14)*, the strongest enemy of all, and He ascended into heaven *(Ephesians 4:8)*, that we too, at the voice of the archangel and the trump of God, shall rise and meet Him in the air, and so shall we ever be with the LORD. *(1 Thessalonians 4:16)*

THE BLOOD

Nothing shall separate us from the love of God, for as Jesus Christ arose a conqueror, we are made more than conquerors through Him that loved us. *(Romans 8:35-39)*

Chapter Eleven

Isaiah 53: Deeper Understanding of His PASSION

Enhancing Our Understanding

Because we are partakers of Yahshua Messiah's suffering, Isaiah 53 is an excellent place to begin our study of the suffering of Christ, and the blood He shed for our sins. Isaiah 53 was written to prophetically speak God's plan into existence, to prepare God's people, and to supply sufficient detail to be able to recognize the Messiah when He came, to announce the coming of a Messiah so great that He would be the perfect Lamb of God. In Him was embodied the perfection that the first Adam in the garden failed to achieve. Jesus fulfilled all of the law given to mankind through Moses; an impossible task, yet He accomplished it.

Hardness of the Heart

The terrible suffering foretold by Isaiah should have made it easy to identify God's suffering Savior, yet they all missed it. Incredible as it seems to us today, a careful look at the prevailing attitudes of Jesus' day: hardness of heart, a strong pharisaical spirit, contentiousness by the religious crowd, refusal to hear Jesus' Words, the spirit of envy that caused them to plot against Him every time He spoke or performed a miracle, all played into missing His coming.

Woe unto you, scribes and Pharisees, hypocrites! For ye pay tithe of mint and anise and cumin, and have omitted the weightier matters of the law, judgment, mercy, and faith: these ought ye to have done, and not to leave the other undone. Ye blind guides, which strain at a gnat, and swallow a camel. Woe unto you, scribes and Pharisees, hypocrites! For ye make clean the outside of the cup and of the platter, but within they are full of extortion and excess. (Matthew 23:23-25)

Verse by Verse Expository of Isaiah 53

Isaiah 53:1 Who hath believed our report? And to whom is the arm of the LORD revealed?

Clearly, the LORD knew that only those who would open their hearts to Him, would recognize His coming.

Isaiah 53:2 For He shall grow up before Him as a tender plant, and as a root out of a dry ground: He hath no form nor comeliness; and when we shall see Him there is no beauty that we should desire Him.

The LORD knew the spiritual mindset at the time of Jesus' birth would be very dry. Jesus was a refreshing drink of cool water. However, one would have to look closely to know Who He was, because He would look like an ordinary man. Invariably, people look on the outward appearance, but our God, YHWH, looks on the heart.

Isaiah 53:3 He is DESPISED and REJECTED of men; a man of SOR-ROWS, and ACQUAINTED with GRIEF: and we hid as it were our faces from Him; He was DESPISED, and we ESTEEMED him not.

The scribes and Pharisees hid their stony hearts, and refused to recognize the very One they claimed to be waiting for.

DESPISED: (*Strong's* 959, bazah) meaning disdain, condemn, think to scorn, vile person.
REJECTED: (*Strong's* 2310, chadel) meaning he that forbears, frail. REJECTED (*Vine's*) states that it means forsak-

en. He endured rejection that we might have acceptance.

ACQUAINTED: (*Strong's* 3045, yada) meaning to have understanding, to know, feel endued with. To be a perfect high priest, Jesus had to experience our grief that we could trust and know His delivering power by faith.

ESTEEMED: (*Vine's*) meaning reckoned.

(For the meaning of SORROWS and GRIEF see verse 4)

Isaiah 53:4 Surely He hath BORNE our GRIEFS, and CARRIED our SORROWS: yet we did esteem Him STRICKEN, SMITTEN of God, and AFFLICTED.

BORNE: (*Strong's* 5375, nacah) meaning to carry, accept, suffer, to bear, carry away.

Carried refers to Jesus' atoning work on the cross.

Borne means to take upon oneself, to carry as a burden: vicarious suffering.

GRIEF: (*Strong's* 2483, choliy) meaning malady, anxiety, calamity, disease.

> (*Vine's*) meaning sicknesses; both spiritual and physical.

CARRIED: (*Strong's* 5445, cabal) meaning to bear, strong labor.

SORROWS: (*Strong's* 4341, makobah) meaning anguish, afflictions, grief, pain and sorrow.

> (*Vine's*) definition is pains, sickness both spiritual and physical. God punished Jesus with all sicknesses. Jesus took our GRIEFS and SORROWS. These are both spiritual and physical sicknesses, so that we would not have to bear them.

STRICKEN: (*Strong's* 5060, naga) meaning violently to strike, punish, to beat, bring down, plague.

SMITTEN: (*Strong's* 5221, nacah) meaning to strike, beat, cast forth, kill, murder, punish, stripes, wounded.

> (*Vine's*) definition is struck down.

AFFLICTED: (*Strong's* 6031, anab) meaning browbeating,

abase self, afflict self, chasten self, defile, force, humble.

Isaiah 53:5 But He was WOUNDED for our TRANSGRESSIONS, He was BRUISED for our INIQUITIES: the CHASTISEMENT of our PEACE was upon Him; and with His STRIPES we are HEALED.

WOUNDED: (*Strong's* 2490, chalal) meaning to wound, to dissolve, to begin by opening a wedge.

(*Vine's*) definition is pierced through.

TRANSGRESSIONS: (*Strong's* 6588, pesha) meaning a revolt (national, moral, or religious), rebellion.

(*Vine's*) definition is wickedness.

By the offense of one (Adam) judgment came on all. *(Romans 5:12-21)*

BRUISED: (*Strong's* 1792, daka) meaning to crumble, beat to pieces, break, crush, destroy, humble, oppress, smite.

INIQUITIES: (*Strong's* 5771, avon) meaning perversity, moral evil, fault, punishment.

(*Vine's*) definition is rebellion.

CHASTISEMENT: (*Strong's* 4148, muwcar) meaning reproof, warning, chastening, correction, discipline, rebuke.

PEACE: (*Strong's* 7965, shalom) meaning safe, well, happy, favor, health, rest, safety, welfare.

STRIPES: (*Strong's* 2250, chaburah) meaning to bruise, hurt, stripe, wound.

(*Vine's*) definition is blows that cut in.

HEALED: (*Strong's* 7495, rapah) meaning to cure, repair, thoroughly make whole, to mend.

Isaiah 53:6 All we like sheep have gone astray; we have turned every one to his own way; and the LORD hath laid on Him the INIQUITY of us all.

INIQUITY: (*Strong's* 5771, avon) meaning perversity, moral evil, fault.

Isaiah 53:7 He was OPPRESSED, and He was AFFLICTED, yet He opened not His mouth: He is brought as a lamb to the slaughter, and as a sheep before her shearers is dumb, so he openeth not His mouth.

OPPRESSED: (*Strong's* 5065, nagas) meaning to harass, tyrannize, distress, a taskmaster, to drive an animal, worker, or debtor.

AFFLICTED: (*Strong's* 6031, anab) meaning browbeating, abase self, afflict self, chasten self, defile, force, humble.

Isaiah 53:8 He was taken from prison and from judgment: and who shall declare His GENERATION? for He was CUT OFF out of the land of the living: for the transgression of my people was He STRICKEN.

GENERATION: (*Strong's* 1755, dowr or dor) meaning posterity, an age or revolution of time.

CUT OFF: (*Strong's* 1504, gazar) meaning to cut down or cut off, to destroy.

STRICKEN: (*Strong's* 5061, nega) meaning a blow, infliction, sore, stricken, stripe, stroke, wound.

Daniel 9:26 And after three score and two weeks shall Messiah be CUT OFF, but not for Himself...

CUT OFF means to be killed.

Isaiah 53:9 And He made His grave with the wicked, and with the rich in His death; because He had done no violence, neither was any deceit in His mouth.

He was the sinless Lamb of God. Being laid in the grave of a rich man was an additional prophetic Word that should have tipped people off that Yahshua (Jesus) was Messiah.

Isaiah 53:10 Yet it pleased the LORD to BRUISE Him; He hath put Him to GRIEF: when thou shalt make His soul an offering for sin, He shall see His seed, He shall prolong His days, and the pleasure of the LORD shall prosper in His hand.

BRUISE: (*Strong's* 1792, daka) meaning to crumble, beat to pieces, break, crush, destroy, humble, oppress, smite.

BRUISE: (*Strong's* 4937, suntribo) meaning to crush, completely, to shatter, broken to shivers. *It (the seed of a woman) shall BRUISE his head, and thou (the serpent) shalt BRUISE his heel. (Genesis 3:15)*

BRUISE: (*Strong's* 7779, shuwph) meaning over whelm, break. Jesus, Himself, fulfilled the prophecy of Genesis 3, that the God of peace shall BRUISE Satan. *(Romans 16:20)*

GRIEF: (*Strong's* 2470, chalah) meaning rubbed or worn, weak, sick, afflicted, grieve, infirmity, put to pain, wounded.

Isaiah 53:11 He shall see of the TRAVAIL of His soul, and shall be SATISFIED: by His knowledge shall My righteous Servant JUSTIFY many; for He shall bear their INIQUITIES.

TRAVAIL: (*Strong's* 5999, amal) meaning wearing effort, worry of body or mind, grievousness, sorrow, toil, trouble, painful.

SATISFIED: (*Strong's* 7646, saba) meaning to sate, fill to satisfaction, have enough, to be full.

JUSTIFY: (*Strong's* 6663, tsadaq) meaning to be or make right in a moral sense, cleanse, clear self, to be or to turn to righteousness.

INIQUITIES: (*Strong's* 5771, avon) meaning perversity, moral evil, fault.

Isaiah 53:12 Therefore will I divide Him a portion with the great, and He shall divide the spoil with the strong; because He hath poured out His soul unto death: and He was numbered with the TRANSGRES-SORS; and He bare the sin of many, and made intercession for the TRANSGRESSORS.

TRANSGRESSORS: (*Strong's* 6586, pasha) meaning to break away from just authority, trespass, apostatize, offend, rebel, revolt, transgress.

The Full Weight of His Suffering

After studying the meanings of the above words in Isaiah 53, the full weight of what Jesus took for us becomes horrifically apparent. It is no wonder that Jesus sweat great drops of blood before His arrest at Gethsemane. He alone understood the full import of the words of the prophecy concerning His PASSION. As the embodiment of the "Word," He fully embraced the extreme suffering: the sorrow, grief, affliction, bruising, travail, oppression, rejection, despising, and chastisement that He would have to suffer. He, alone, grasped the depth of our transgression and iniquity that He must bear for the wickedness of mankind.

Yahshua Messiah was despised, disdained, condemned, scorned and treated like a vile person. He bore our rejection, was violently struck, punished, beaten, pierced through, smitten, wounded, abased, chastised, defiled, humiliated and plagued. The sinless Son of God took upon Himself our afflictions and carried, accepted and bore our burdens, griefs, pains and sorrows, through vicarious suffering for our sins. He was murdered for you and me.

He endured this strong affliction in order to intimately know the full extent of sorrow, anguish, malady, anxiety, calamity and every disease known to mankind. He travailed and took all this for our national and religious rebellion, revolt, wickedness, perversity, moral failure, faults, transgressions and offenses. He was bruised, hurt, beat to pieces, punished, broken, crushed, shattered, overwhelmed and put to pain to set us free.

He bore our destruction, oppression, reproof, discipline and rebuke. He carried the stripes on His back that should be ours. He was harassed, tyrannized, distressed, cut off, driven like an animal and a debtor. He bore our infirmities and sicknesses, spiritually, mentally, physically and materially.

Yahshua the Messiah, Jesus the Christ of Nazareth, endured this horror to satisfy, fulfill and satiate God's wrath, to right us morally, cleanse us, to clear the slate against us, and to wipe out our trespasses, rebellion, revolt and wickedness. In turn, He provided us with safety, healing, deliverance, happiness, favor, health, rest, and welfare. He repaired the breach between God and man, tore down the wall of separation between us, mended and thoroughly made whole our relationship with our Creator. Only He, being perfect, could oversee His own sacrifice.

Sweating Blood

Medical science has documented cases of humans sweating blood under extreme duress. We all know sweat pours off under intense emotional pressure. In the sweat of our faces we have brought forth thorns and thistles, for the ground was cursed. We are delivered from this curse through His redeeming blood. *(Genesis 3:17-19)*

...was as it were great DROPS OF BLOOD. (Luke 22:44)

Guilt and Shame

Jesus died for the guilt and the shame of our sins. The Jews were looking for a Messiah who would take back Judah from the Romans by force. Herod and the Sanhedrin greatly feared Jesus, because the people loved and followed Him. He was perceived as a threat to their positions given them by Roman rule. They never grasped Jesus' true purpose because of the hardness of their hearts, fear of losing their positions, and the envy that consumed them.

Redeemed from the Curse

Jesus had to be crucified: to redeem us from the curse of the law. Redeem (*Strong's* 1805, exagorazo) means to buy up, ransom, rescue from loss, to purchase. God spared not His own Son *(Romans 8:32)* that we might be saved.

Christ has REDEEMED us from the CURSE OF THE LAW, being made a curse for us...that the blessings of Abraham might come on the gentiles. (Galatians 3:12-14)

Chapter Twelve
The Betrayal

The sorrow and suffering that our Savior took for us is most painfully portrayed through the kiss of a friend. When we say that we are the friend or servant of God, and we betray Him through disobedience, or failure to show our love for Him by keeping His commandments, it is just as painful to Him. Yet, in His mercy, He continues to love us.

The Cup of Suffering

He took the CUP of suffering that we might drink from the well of living water. *(John 4:10)* **The CUP which My father hath given Me, shall I not drink it: (John 18:11)**

Betrayed By A Kiss

The KISS of Judas is the worst betrayal in history, accomplished through a sign of love and friendship. *(Luke 22:48; Matthew 26:49; Mark 14:45)* Judas was, at that time, one of the twelve disciples, someone Jesus entrusted to handle the money. **Faithful are the wounds of a friend; but the KISSES of an enemy are deceitful. (Proverbs 27:6)**

Acquainted With Grief

YHWH, our God, put Yahshua Messiah to GRIEF. *(Isaiah 53:10)* Definitions of GRIEF follow:

GRIEF: (*Vine's*) meaning sicknesses, both spiritual and physical.

GRIEF: (*Strong's* 2483, choliy) malady, anxiety, disease, calamity.

GRIEF: (*Strong's* 2470, chalah) meaning to be weak, sick

and afflicted, grievous, put to pain, be wounded, woman in travail.

Sorrow

SORROW: (*Strong's* 4341, makobah) anguish, grief, sickness, both spiritual and physical, affliction, pain. Our griefs and sorrows were carried by our Savior. *He hath borne our GRIEFS and carried our SORROWS. (Isaiah 53:3-4)*

SORROW: (*Strong's* 3077, lupe) meaning grief, heaviness, sadness. *He found them sleeping for SORROW. (Luke 22:45)*

SORROW: (*Strong's* 4036, perilupos) meaning grieved all around, intensely sad, almost dying of sorrow. *...exceeding SORROWFUL unto death. (Matthew 14:24)*

SORROW: (*Strong's* 6089, etseb) meaning grievous, usually painful toil, labor.
...cursed is the ground for thy (Adam) *sake; in SORROW shalt thou eat of it. (Genesis 3:17)*

SORROW: (*Strong's* 6093, itstabown) meaning toil, labor, pain. *I will greatly multiply thy* (Eve) *SORROW. (Genesis 3:16)*

SORROWFUL: (*Strong's* 3076, lupeo) meaning to distress, cause grief, be in heaviness, to be sorry. *He took with Him Peter and the two sons of Zebedee and began to be SORROWFUL and very HEAVY. (Matthew 26:37)*

SORROWFUL: (*Strong's* 4036, perilupos) meaning intensely, exceedingly sad, grieved all around. *Then He said unto them, My soul is exceeding SORROWFUL, even unto death... (Matthew 26:38)*

Heavy

HEAVY: (*Strong's* 85, ademoneo) meaning to be in distress

of mind; full of heaviness. Jesus suffered emotionally to the point of death, before any physical suffering began, so that an angel had to come and strengthen Him. *(Luke 22:43)*

I Am

Six hundred men, plus chief priests and others who had come to arrest Jesus fell backward, knocked down by the power of God, through the spoken Name "*I Am.*" This Name represents the eternal, uncreated God, the Holy One of Israel. How easy it would have been for Jesus to simply walk away from the agony yet to come. *(John 18:5)*

False Witnesses

There were false witnesses at the trial against Jesus, that our loins could be girt about with truth. *(Ephesians 6:14; Psalm 27:12; Matthew 26:60-61)*

Two Trials

Jesus received two trials. One was uniquely Jewish, one was distinctly Roman. We will experience two trials, as well. The one on earth determines if we will follow the true God. All of life is a test. The other, if we choose not to follow the way of righteousness, is known as the Great White Throne Judgment. We are often tried by men on earth, but the trial that determines our eternal destiny is the one we should be concerned about. Our choices on earth determine the outcome, for everything is being recorded in heaven. Those who receive Jesus now, have their names written in the Lamb's Book of Life.

Three stages:
Jewish Trial
1. Examination before Annas. *(John 18:12-23)*
2. Hearing before Caiaphas and Sanhedrin with false witnesses. *(Matthew 26:57-64)*
3. Trial: Chief priests and elders took counsel and sentenced

Jesus to death, bound Him and delivered Him to Pilate. *(Matthew 27:1-2)*

Roman Trial
1. Examination by Pilate. *(Luke 23:1-7)*
2. Interrogation by Herod. *(Luke 23:8-11)*
3. Meeting with Pilate before crowd and sentencing. Pilate washed his hands of the matter, but again the chief priests and elders persuaded the multitude to request Barabbas' release and Jesus' death. *"His blood be on us, and on our children,"* they cried. *(Matthew 27:15-31; Luke 23:13-25)*[1]

Two High Priests

Annas was Caiaphas' father-in-law. Annas was deposed by the Romans, but he was technically still high priest. Thus, Jesus was brought before two high priests.

"For the absolutely sinless One to be subjected to a trial conducted by sinful men was in itself a deep humiliation. To be tried by such men, under such circumstances made it infinitely worse. Greedy, serpent-like, vindictive Annas; rude, sly, hypocritical Caiaphas; crafty, superstitious, self-seeking Pilate; and immoral, ambitious, superficial Herod Antipas; these were His judges!"[1]

Fear in the Sanhedrin

The Sanhedrin had seventy members: twenty-three consti-tuted a quorum. There were three groups: priests, teachers of the law and elders. The perceived threat of violence was enough to hold the trial, but the witnesses lied and said that He threatened to destroy the temple. *(John 2:18-21; Mark 14:59)*

Blasphemy

Blasphemy is dishonoring God by diminishing His glory or

claiming rights God alone possesses. The following are reasons used to accuse Jesus of blasphemy.

1. Jesus claimed He would be seated at the right hand of God, a position only God's Son could hold.

2. One as apparently helpless as Jesus could not be the Messiah they expected. They were expecting a Messiah who would take over the government and defeat the Romans.

3. Jews believed God alone had the right to enthrone Messiah. Jesus' claims enraged them.

Interrogation

Jesus' response to interrogation is that He clearly claims to be the Messiah.

...Thou hast said: nevertheless I say unto you, Hereafter shall ye see the Son of man sitting on the right hand of power, and coming in the clouds of heaven. (Matthew 26:64)

Old Testament prophecies fulfilled:

...the Son of man came with the clouds of heaven, and came to the Ancient of days... (Daniel 7:13)

The LORD (YHWH) *said unto my LORD* (Adon, master, Jesus), *Sit Thou at My right hand, until I make Thine enemies Thy footstool. (Psalm 110:1)*

Chapter Thirteen
The Passion

Jesus Abused Twice

1. By the religious crowd. *(Matthew 26:67-68)*
2. By Pilate's soldiers. *(Mark 15:19)*

Blindfolded

This was mockingly done because of a Jewish test that the Messiah would need neither eyes nor ears to identify people.

Scarlet Robe

They stripped Him, placed on Him a scarlet robe, and mocked His kingship, that we might be kings and priests. *(Matthew 27:28)*

The Scepter

The soldiers of the governor humiliated Jesus and mocked His claim that He was a king by placing a scepter, symbol of authority and power made of a reed, in His hand. *(Mark 15:19)*

Hit On His Head With a Reed

To maximize His suffering and humiliation, and to prove His weakness and inability to defend Himself, they took the reed they had given Him and struck Him on the head and shoulders, driving the thorns in deeper.

Mocked Three Times

Before Jesus got to the cross, He was mocked three times and denied three times, that we might be empowered to resist pride, rebellion and hardness of heart through humility.

1. Caiaphas and the chief priests mocked Him. *(Matthew 26:67-68)*
2. Herod's soldiers mocked Him. *(Luke 23:10-11)*
3. Pilate's men mocked Him. *(John 19:1-3)*

Mocked Again

Crowned with thorns, adorned with a robe of purple, they mockingly kneeled before Him, hit Him with the reed they had placed in His hand as a scepter, and yelled, "***Hail, King of the Jews.***" *(John 19:1-3)* They spit upon Him and shouted, "***Prophesy unto us, Thou Christ, who is he that smote Thee.***" *(Matthew 26:67-68; Isaiah 50:6; Mark 14:65; Psalm 22:7-8)*

MOCKED: (*Strong's* 1702, empaizo) meaning to jeer at, deride. *(Matthew 27:29, 31, 41; 27:29-30; Mark 15:20, 31;15:19; Luke 18:32; 22:63; 23:11, 36)*

Accused

He was accused of being a criminal, that we might be justif ied by grace through faith. *(Romans 3:24-25)*

ACCUSED: (*Strong's* 2722, kategoreo) meaning to charge with some offense. *(Luke 23:10)*

Vehemently Accused

Vehemently (*Strong's* 2159, eutonos) means fiercely, mightily.

And the chief priests and scribes stood and VEHEMENTLY accused Him. And Herod with his men of war set Him at naught and mocked Him… (Luke 23:10)

Blows to His Face

There were blows to His face, that we might have healing for our offenses and wounded hearts; interesting to note that this was done by the religious crowd. Of further note are the various intensities and kinds of blows His face and body received. Below is a sample of the various Greek words used to describe His abuse.

BUFFET: (*Strong's* 2852, kolaphizo) to rap with fist. *(Mark 14:65)*

STRIKE: (*Strong's* 906, ballo) violent, intense, thrust, throw. *(Mark 14:65)*

SMOTE: (Strong's 4474, rhapizo) to slap, smite. *(Matthew 26:67)*

SMOTE: (*Strong's* 3317, paio) to sting as a scorpion; strike, hit. *(Matthew 26:68)*

SMITEST: (*Strong's* 1194, dero) to thrash, beat, scourge. *(John 18:23)*

STRUCK: (*Strong's* 5180, tupto) to pummel with repeated blows with stick or fist, beat, smite, strike, wound. *(Luke 22:64)*

STRUCK: (*Strong's* 3960, patasso) to knock with a weapon or fatally smite, strike. *(John 18:22)*

SLAPPED CHEEK: denotes feelings, deliberate humiliation.

Creation Mocks the Creator

God's own creation, man, mocked His Son: they esteemed Him not. *(Luke 22:63)*

Guards Spit

The guards spit and kept on SPITTING, heaping scorn on Him. This action was prophesied in the Old Testament. *...I hid not my face from shame and SPITTING... (Isaiah 50:6)*

Plucked His Beard

Plucking out His beard was another form of humiliation. He was humbled that we might be exalted. *(James 1:9)* He led captivity captive. PLUCKING out the beard was prophesied in the Old Testament. *I gave My back to the smiters, and My cheeks to those who PLUCKED off the hair... (Isaiah 50:6)*

Reviled

The word reviled comes from the word blaphemeo, meaning to blaspheme, rail on, speak evil of. *(Psalm 109:25)*

Set At Naught

The phrase "set at naught" means that He was treated with great contempt. *(Luke 23:11)*

Envy

ENVY: (*Strong's* 5355, phthonos) meaning ill-will, spite, jealousy. ***...Pilate...knew that the chief priests had delivered Him for ENVY. (Mark 15:10)***

Dumb Before His Shearers

The Lamb of God was dumb before His shearers, that we might have an answer for every accusation raised against us. *(Isaiah 53:7; Matthew 26:63)* He did not try to justify, or deliver, or defend Himself. He said nothing, though He could have summoned twelve legions of angels *(Matthew 26:53)*, so that when we stand before our accusers, the Holy Spirit will give us the words to speak. *(Matthew 27:37; 1 Peter 3:15; Luke 12:11-12)*

Mocked Yet Again

While on the cross they mocked Him saying that if He was the Son of God, then He should come down off the cross and save Himself. Others He saved, they jeered at Him, yet Himself He could not save. *(Isaiah 50:6; Luke 18:33)*

Visage

Jesus' body and face were so MARRED that He did not even look human. He endured the penalty and was reckoned and regarded as guilty of our sins. This was the ultimate sacrifice. The suffering and physical disfigurement were unparalleled. His body bore every disease known to man as He hung on the cross. This was prophesied in Isaiah hundreds of years before.

As many were astonished at thee; His VISAGE was so MARRED more than any man, and his form more than the sons of men... (Isaiah 52:14)

Back

The BACK symbolized rebellion against God and His Torah. Yahshua willingly took this beating to set us free. *I gave My BACK to the smiters... (Isaiah 50:6)*

Scourged

The flagellum (Latin word) was a terrible instrument *(Mark 15:15)*, with thick strips of leather platted with bits of metal or bone into a chain, designed to tear away the flesh, and leave it hanging in bleeding shreds. The Flagellum (*Strong's* 5417, phragelloo) is taken from the presumed equivalent of the Latin flagellum, meaning to whip or lash as a public punishment. Under Roman law there was no maximum number of strokes, unlike Jewish law. *...and by His STRIPES we are healed. (Isaiah 53:5; 1 Peter 2:24)*

Administering the STRIPES was referred to as "being examined." Thirteen went to the back, thirteen to each shoulder, for a total of thirty-nine. This number was set in order not to break the law, which allowed only forty, in case of a miscount. Many men died from the stripes alone. When the flagellum struck it would wrap around the body as it brutally tore and pulled away the flesh, often exposing the bone.

It has been stated by doctors that there are thirty-nine categories of disease. Collectively, the stripes that Jesus took on His back healed all our diseases. This is discussed fully in the next book in this series of three: *Stripes*.

Chapter Fourteen

The Passion of the Cross

He Bore the Cross

Yahshua (Jesus) bore the cross. *(John 19:17)* He bore the weight that so easily beset us. *(Hebrews 12:1)* Now we can roll the weight of our cares onto Him, for He cares for us. *(1 Peter 5:7)* He carried all our sorrows. *(Isaiah 53:4)*

Crucified Outside Gates of City

Jesus was crucified outside the gates of the city. This was part of the rejection and extreme shame of the cross. *(Hebrews 13:12)*

Hung On A Cross

Being "lifted up" *(John 12:32)* meant crucifixion, which was a "Roman" form of execution. Romans had to be involved in the crucifixion to fulfill this prophecy. The height of the cross was no more than one or two feet off the ground, so that dogs and wild beasts could feed on the corpses. Crucifixion was done in very public places such as a crossroads for maximum exposure and humiliation.

The sedecula was a small peg or block fixed midway up the vertical beam to provide a seat, preventing premature collapse, and deliberately prolonging the agony. The scarcity of references to crucifixion in literature and the Bible is probably because there was such revulsion, disgust, reproach and degradation associated with this form of punishment. Writers probably did not want to defile or disgrace their work by referring to it. The cross was considered the worst of human obscenities.

Hung On A Tree

He became a curse for us by hanging on a TREE.

Cursed is every one that hangeth on a TREE. (Galatians 3:13)

He bare our sins in His own body on the TREE. (1 Peter 2:24)

Lots Cast

At the foot of the cross, the guards divided Jesus' garments among themselves, but recognized the value of the seamless coat he wore. Rather than tear it, they gambled for it. The following prophecy, given hundreds of years before by King David, is one of the most convincing proofs that Jesus was Messiah. *(John 19:24)* **They PART MY GARMENTS among them, and CAST LOTS upon My VESTURE. (Psalm 22:18)**

Naked

Jesus hung on the cross naked, shamefully exposed. Shame came into the Garden of Eden when Adam and Eve discovered they were naked through sin. *(Genesis 3:7)* Our shame comes when our sin is not covered by the blood of the Lamb, the saving knowledge of Jesus. He was naked on the cross, that we might be clothed in robes of righteousness.

Shame Worse Than Pain

Personal humiliation, public nakedness on high ground, degradation, obscenity, reproach, and disgust of the cross were all borne by Jesus, to take away both our guilt and shame. *(Hebrews 13:2, 12-13)* He bore our shame, that we might share His glory. When Adam and Eve knew they were naked, they hid from the LORD. Jesus suffered public nakedness, unable to hide from the wrath against sinful mankind. He was exposed and naked for us, that we might receive the covering of His robe of righteousness. *(Isaiah 61:10)*

Crucified With Sinners

The sinless Son of God hung in shame between two sinners. One reviled Him, the other defended Him. The first went to everlasting death, while the other was taken to paradise. *(Isaiah 53:12; Matthew 27:38)*

Numbered With Transgressors

Isaiah prophesies that Yahshua will be numbered with the TRANSGRESSORS (*Strong's* 6586, pasha) meaning to break away from just authority, trespass, rebel, revolt. He was numbered with them for our rebellion. *(Isaiah 53:12)*

> ***And with Him they crucify two thieves, the one on His right hand, and the other on His left. (Mark 15:27-28)***

Derided

Jesus was DERIDED: (Strong's 1592, ekmukterizo) meaning sneered outright at.

> **He** *saved others; let Him save Himself, if He be Christ… (Luke 23:35)*

Gall

Jesus refused to drink the GALL: (*Strong's* 5521, chose) meaning a soothing or pain relieving agent, bile, a bitter poison. He refused to be bitter. The vinegar mixed with gall was probably laced with a bitter narcotic to deaden the pain, a common practice. He refused the drink with gall that would have dulled His senses, so that He might know the full extent of suffering for us on the cross.

> ***They gave Him vinegar to drink mingled with GALL. (Matthew 27:34)***

> ***…in the GALL of bitterness. (Acts 8:23)***

THE BLOOD

Forgiveness

When Yahshua forgave His murderers it released the power of the Holy Spirit in the earth. This forgiveness enabled Him to be raised from the dead *(Acts 2:24)*. When Jesus forgave from the cross, He Himself could then be the first born raised from the dead *(Colossians 1:18)*, that we, too, could be raised up to sit together with Him in heavenly places. *(Ephesians 2:6)* **Father, FORGIVE THEM; for they know not what they do. (Luke 23:34)**

Thirst Quenched with Vinegar

In Jesus' day, vinegar was soured wine, plain and unmixed. This was given to Jesus when He said, ***"I thirst!"*** *(John 19:28-30)* This was simultaneously spoken by the high priest on the temple mount. He took the bitter fruit of the vine, that He might bear much good fruit through us.

Railed

His accusers RAILED on Him, with accusations based on false assumptions. God did not deliver His Son, in order that He could offer salvation to all who would receive it. Because He did not come down from the cross, they walked away satisfied that He was not the Messiah. This is the worst His enemies could say. It is precisely because He did not come down from the cross that we believe on Him. If only our enemies could say we spent our lives helping others and trusting God. Satan was using these men to taunt Jesus into actually coming down (another temptation motivated by Satan). Jesus did something greater than coming down from the cross. He rose from the dead, and they still did not believe Him.

And they that passed by railed on Him, wagging their heads and saying, Ah, Thou that destroyest the temple and buildest it in three days, Save Thyself, and come down from the cross. Likewise also the chief priests mocking said among themselves with the scribes,

He saved others; Himself He cannot save. Let Christ the King of Israel descend now from the cross, that we may see and believe. And they that were crucified with Him reviled Him. (Mark 15:29-32)

King David prophesied that this would occur. *All they that see me laugh me to scorn: they shoot out the lip, they shake the head, saying, He trusted on the LORD that He would deliver Him... (Psalm 22:7-8)*

Darkness

The darkness on the earth during the crucifixion reflects the darkness of Christ's soul as He suffered divine wrath *(Romans 5:9)* for sinners. *(Luke 23:44)* The hideousness of sin being borne by the sinless Son of God could only be expressed and symbolized by the darkness over the land and the people. Speculation continues by scientists that it could have been an eclipse, or other coincidental weather phenomenon.

And it shall come to pass in that day, saith the LORD God, that I will cause the sun to go down at noon, and I will darken the earth in the clear day: And I will turn your feasts into mourning, and all your songs into lamentation; and I will bring up sackcloth upon all loins, and baldness upon every head; and I will make it as the MOURNING OF AN ONLY SON, and the end thereof as a bitter day. (Amos 8:9-10)

Forsaken

Yahshua's plaintive cry from the cross is really the fulfillment of David's prophetic Psalm concerning the Messiah. This Psalm begins with Jesus' words from the cross, and ends with His last words.

MY GOD, MY GOD, WHY HAST THOU FORSAKEN ME?...All they that see Me laugh Me to scorn: they shoot out the lip, they shake the head, saying, He trusted on the LORD that He would deliver Him: let Him deliver Him, seeing He delighted in Him...Thou hast brought Me into the dust of death. For dogs have compassed Me: the assembly of the wicked have inclosed Me: they pierced My hands and My feet...They part My garments among them, and cast lots upon My vesture...that HE HATH DONE THIS. (Psalm 22)

Notice the final words, HE HATH DONE THIS. In Hebrew this is really, IT IS FINISHED! Jesus final words. Some scholars believe that He shouted the first and last words of this Psalm, and quietly spoke the rest in between. Using the Name God in this instance, instead of His usual "Father" indicates that something has transpired. Something is different. The Righteous Judge is punishing Him. Still, He calls Him "My God," still reaching out to Him. The crowds that had once followed Jesus forsook Him, Judas betrayed Him, the disciples hid, Peter denied Him, and finally God forsook Him.

The punishment for sin is separation from God. This was the worst part of Yahshua's death. You and I do not have to suffer separation from God because Jesus took wrath for us. *(Roman's 5:9)* He laid the foundation for our deliverance from spiritual and physical corruption. He secured the blessing, and took away the curse. He was forsaken so that God would never leave or forsake us. *(Hebrews 3:5)* The fulfillment of a millennia of prophecy is that **God's wrath is quenched through His Son's sacrifice** and He is SATISFIED.

He shall see of the travail of His soul, and shall be SATIS-FIED... (Isaiah 53:11)

Chapter Fifteen

The Finished Work of the Cross

Through Yahshua's (Jesus') death we have reconciliation, redemption, righteousness, sanctification and salvation. Jesus' ministry on earth was **finished**, the old covenant law had been fulfilled. Even in death, Jesus was in control of when He gave up His life. He had certain things to accomplish before He could release His spirit from His body. He resumed calling God His Father. *It is finished* is a victory cry, a triumphant exclamation! The redemption was complete. He commended (*Strong's* 3908, paratithemi) Himself into His Father's hands. COMMEND means to deposit as a trust for protection, commit to the keeping of.

Veil Torn

Upon Jesus death, the veil separating the Inner Court of the temple from the Holy of Holies, was torn in two. In the natural this would be impossible. Solomon's temple was 30 cubits high, but Herod had increased it to 40 cubits, according to the historian, Josephus. The "veil" was between **60 and 90 feet high**, and **several feet thick**. Only God Himself could have torn the veil in two, from top to bottom. This act alone should have awakened the religious Jews, but their eyes were still blinded to the truth.

The veil represented separation of man from God, through sin. Only the high priest was able to enter beyond this veil once a year. At the moment of Christ's death, this veil was torn in two, revealing that the perfect sacrifice was made and there was no longer any separation between man and God. The veil symbolized Jesus' flesh, torn, to open a way to YHWH, our God, through Him.
(Hebrews 9:7, 28; Exodus 30:10; Matthew 27:51; Mark 27:38)

Earthquake

The earthquake at Jesus' death cracked the ground, moving aside the lid on the container holding the Ark of the Covenant, buried in a chamber directly below the cross where Jesus hung. Additionally, it caused stones to roll away from certain tombs, and saints arose from their graves after Jesus' resurrection, and were seen in Jerusalem. *(Matthew 27:51-52)* Death lost its grip on many captives. The earth itself was shaken to its very foundation, for Jesus was the Chief Cornerstone. *(Ephesians 2:20)* **The earth did quake, and the rocks rent. (Matthew 27:51)**

There was another earthquake when the angel of the LORD descended from heaven and rolled away the stone from the door of the sepulcher where Jesus was buried, and sat upon it. *(Matthew 28:2)*

Side Pierced By Spear

He gave His flesh for the fulfillment of the law *(1 Peter 4:1)*, to break the curse of the law that separated us from God. *(Galatians 3:13)* Thus, at Pentecost, 40 days later, the Holy Spirit was poured out on all flesh. *(Acts 2:17)*

Being PIERCED in the side *(John 19:34)* was the fulfillment of another prophecy that cannot be denied, for usually guards broke the legs without any piercing. **...They shall look upon Me Whom they have PIERCED... (Zechariah 12:10)**

Blood on the Mercy Seat

Jesus was probably speared on the left side under the fifth rib, the location of the spleen. The water separated on top of the heavier blood. Probably three to five units of blood were spilled. When the rocks split in the earthquake, this created an opening on the left side of the cross, where the blood splashed down on the mercy seat of the Ark of the Covenant, buried directly below 600 years before, in Jeremiah's Grotto, awaiting the perfect fulfillment of Messiah's blood sacrifice.[2] This reveals the mercy and careful forethought of our loving God.

Innocent Blood

Jesus' innocent blood began to be shed at Gethsemane when He sweat blood, and continued until after His death. The infinite power of the blood of Christ has not even begun to be comprehended by finite man. His precious blood:

1. Forgives the sins of those who repent, accept His forgiveness, and believe. It brings redemption. *(Ephesians 1:7)* **For this is my blood of the New Testament, which is shed for many for the remission of sins. (Matthew 26:28)**

2. Ransoms all believers from the power of Satan and evil powers.

> *...the church of God, which He hath purchased with His own blood. (Acts 20:28)*
>
> *...ye know that ye were not redeemed with corruptible things. (1 Peter 1:18-19)*
>
> *Thou wast slain, and hast redeemed us to God by Thy blood... (Revelation 5:9)*
>
> *And they overcame Him by the blood of the Lamb... (Revelation 12:11)*

> *Who hath delivered us from the power of darkness, and hath translated us into the kingdom of His dear Son. (Colossians 1:13)*

3. Justifies all who believe in Him. His shed blood makes salvation a possibility.

> *…Whom God hath sent forth to be a propitiation through faith in His blood, to declare His righteousness for the remission of sins… (Romans 3:24-25)*

4. Cleanses believer's consciences that they might serve God without guilt, in full assurance.

> *How much more shall the blood of Christ, Who through the eternal Spirit offered Himself without spot to God, purge your conscience from dead works to serve the living God? (Hebrews 9:14)*

> *Let us draw near with a true heart in full assurance of faith, having our hearts sprinkled* (with Christ's blood) *from an evil conscience. (Hebrews 10:22)*

5. Sanctifies God's people.

> *Wherefore Jesus also, that He might sanctify the people with His own blood, suffered without the gate. (Hebrews 13:12)*

> *…the blood of Jesus Christ His Son cleanseth us from all sin. (1 John 1:7)*

6. Opens the way (access) for believers to come directly before God through Christ in order to receive grace, mercy, help and salvation.

> *Wherefore He is able also to save them to the uttermost that come unto God by Him, seeing He ever liveth to make intercession for them. (Hebrews 7:25)*

> *Having therefore, brethren, boldness to enter into the holiest by the blood of Jesus. (Hebrews 10:19)*

But now in Christ Jesus ye who sometimes were far off are made nigh by the blood of Christ. (Ephesians 2:13)

7. Guarantee of all promises of the NEW eternal COVENANT.

Of how much sorer punishment, suppose ye, shall he be thought worthy, Who hath trodden under foot the Son of God, and hath counted the blood of the covenant, wherewith he was sanctified, an unholy thing, and hath done despite unto the Spirit of grace? (Hebrews 10:29)

For this is My blood of the NEW TESTAMENT. (Matthew 26:28)

This cup is the NEW TESTAMENT in My blood which is shed for you. (Luke 22:20)

And to Jesus the mediator of the NEW COVENANT, and to the blood of sprinkling, that speaketh better things than that of Abel. (Hebrews 12:24)

In Whom we have redemption through His blood, the forgiveness of sins, according to the riches of His grace...(Ephesians 1:7)

8. The blood saves, reconciles, purifies, there is power in the blood to continually cleanse us from sin. Jesus is our Passover Lamb. *(Exodus 12:7-8; 1 Corinthians 5:7; Hebrews 7:25; 10:22; 1 John 1:7)* We are forbidden to drink any other blood, yet we are to symbolically consume His blood in observing the new covenant. *(John 6:53-56)*

9. Is central to the New Testament concept of redemption.

79

The cup of blessing which we bless, is it not the communion of the blood of Christ: (1 Corinthians 10:16)

But now in Christ Jesus ye who sometimes were far off are made nigh by the blood of Christ. (Ephesians 2:13)

Elect according to the foreknowledge of God the Father, through sanctification of the Spirit, unto obedience and sprinkling of the blood of Jesus Christ... (1 Peter 1:2)

...These are they which came out of great tribulation, and have washed their robes, and made them white in the blood of the Lamb. (Revelation 7:14)

10. Shed blood removes our sins and reconciles us with God.

...by the obedience of One shall many be made righteous. (Romans 5:19)

And being found in fashion as a man, He humbled Himself, and became obedient unto death, even the death of the cross. (Philippians 2:8; Leviticus 16)

11. He died as a ransom to free us from sins committed under the first covenant.

And for this cause He is the mediator of the New Testament, that by means of death, for the redemption of the transgressions that were under the first testament, they which are called might receive the promise of eternal inheritance. (Hebrews 9:15)

12. He entered the most holy place with His own blood, once for all, and obtained our redemption with His blood.

> *Neither by the blood of goats and calves, but by His own blood He entered in once into the holy place, having obtained eternal redemption for us. (Hebrews 9:12)*

13. We overcome by the blood. *(Revelation 12:11)*

14. Wash in the blood during the tribulation. *(Revelation 7:14)*

14. Was a trespass offering. *(Leviticus 7:2)*

15. Was a peace offering. *(Exodus 29:20-21)*

16. Was atonement for sins. *(Leviticus 16:14-15, 18-19, 27; 17:11)*

17. Took our judgment. *(Ezekiel 16:38; Revelation 16:6)*

18. Took our oppression and cruelty. *(Habakkuk 2:12)*

19. Took our guilt. *(Leviticus 20:9; 2 Samuel 1:16; Ezekiel 18:13)*

20. Remission of sins, sin offering, atonement. *(Leviticus 4; 8:15; Exodus 29:12; 30:10)*

> *For this is My blood of the New Testament, which is shed for many for the remission of sins. (Matthew 26:28)*

> *Then Jesus said unto them, Verily, verily, I say unto you, Except ye eat the flesh of the Son of man, and drink His blood, ye have no life in you, Whoso eateth My flesh, and drinketh My blood, hath eternal life; and I will raise him up at the last day. (John 6:53)*

> *...to feed the church of God, which He hath purchased with His own blood. (Acts 20:28)*

> *Being justified freely by His grace through the redemption that is in Christ Jesus: Whom God hath set forth to be a propitiation through faith in His blood, to declare His righteousness for the remission of sins that are past, through the forbearance of God... (Romans 3:24)*

> *Much more then, being now justified by His blood, we shall be saved from wrath through Him...by Whom we have now received the atonement. (Romans 5:9-11)*

> *The cup of blessing which we bless, is it not the communion of the blood of Christ? (1 Corinthians 10:16)*

21. His blood makes us perfect (complete), and righteous.

> *...our LORD Jesus, that Great Shepherd of the sheep, through the blood of the everlasting covenant, Make you perfect (complete) in every good work... (Hebrews 13:20-21)*

> *...through faith in His blood, to declare His righteousness for the remission of sins... (Romans 3:25)*

22. New covenant ratified with shed blood. Jesus, mediator of new covenant. *(Hebrews 9:15)*

> *But now hath He obtained a more excellent ministry, by how much also He is the mediator of a better covenant, which was established upon better promises. (Hebrews 8:6)*

23. Protected by the blood. Evil passes over us through the applying of the blood of the Lamb of God to the doorposts of our hearts.

...take you a lamb...and kill the Passover. And ye shall take a bunch of hyssop, and dip it in the blood that is in the basin, and strike the lintel and the two side posts with the blood... (Exodus 12:21-22)

Three Who Bear Witness on Earth

The Spirit, the water, the blood, and they all agree. *(1 John 5:8)*

No Bones Broken

No bones were broken during Jesus' crucifixion, for His sinless body became a bridge between God and man.

The Water and the Blood

Sacrificed animal parts were washed in the water of the laver in the outer court of the temple. When Jesus' side was pierced, both blood and water came out. The water that came out of Jesus' side represents the washing of the Word. *(Ephesians 5:26)* The first high priest, Aaron, had his ear, thumb and toe anointed with blood. *(Leviticus 8:23)* Jesus had thorns placed on His head, causing blood to run on to His ears, and He had nails driven through His hands and feet from which His blood flowed, that the Old Testament shadow-picture of a high priest could be fulfilled in Him.

There is life in the blood. *(Leviticus 17:11)* The blood of Jesus continuously cleanses and justifies us. *(Ephesians 1:7)* We have redemption through His blood, forgiveness of sins. Being now justified by His blood, we are saved from the wrath we deserve. *(Romans 5:9)* The blood of Christ purges (cleanses) us from dead works. *(Hebrews 9:14)* We are sanctified through the blood of Jesus once for all. *(Hebrews 10:9)* His blood speaks, it shouts the victory He won for us *(Genesis 4:10)*, for His shed blood released us from Satan's power.

THE BLOOD

> *...that through death He might destroy him that had the power of death, that is, the devil and deliver them who through fear of death were all their lifetime subject to bondage. (Hebrews 2:14-15)*

Sacrificed Innocent Lamb of God

He became sin for us. He took our wrath and judgment, that we might live with Him forever. *...while we were yet sinners Christ died for us. (Romans 5:8)*

Sinless Blood

Jesus, the last Adam, had blood that was unique, for it was not sin-filled. He was not born of Adam's blood, but was fathered by God Himself, and born of a virgin, *(Matthew 1:22)* yet His body was from the sinful flesh of His mother. No one with the first Adam's blood could have offered himself for our redemption and ransom, because all human blood had sin. We know from scripture that life is in the blood *(Leviticus 17:11)*, and from medical science that blood type is conveyed entirely by the father. The Messiah was safe in His mother's womb because blood cells and bacteria are too big to pass through the placenta to the unborn child. **(3)

With no blood passing from mother to child, it became necessary for YHWH to place His seed by the Holy Spirit into a virgin to prevent wicked blood from passing to His son. The father's protoplasmic seed is made of fluid and plasma (water and blood). *(1 John 5:6)* **(4) Thus, only Jesus could sanctify us through His own blood and redeem us. Faith in His blood brings us salvation. *(Revelation 5:9)* Because His blood was sinless, it did more than cover sin; it literally did away with it.

The last Adam, Jesus, had undefiled sinless blood *(1 Corinthians 15:45)*, enabling Him to become our high priest *(Romans 5:9)*, and we are gloriously born again when we receive Yahshua as our Messiah.

While man's blood cleanses his own body of impurities, the Messiah's blood cleanses man from sin. **(5) Sin circulates throughout man's body, soul and spirit, but Jesus provides us with a blood cleaning procedure we cannot afford to miss. Once His sinless blood has purified the spirit of a man, the man becomes part of the "body" of Messiah.

Chapter Sixteen

Burial and Resurrection of the Messiah

Spices

Myrrh was given to Jesus at His birth and used on Him at His burial. *(John 19:40)* Myrrh (*Strong's* 3463, muron) was a spice that represented death. Mary, a follower of Jesus, brought an alabaster box of fragrant ointment and broke it to anoint Jesus for His burial. She gave her most costly, precious possession. (One hundred pound weight, about seventy-five pounds, was worth thousands of dollars.) It refers to the costliness of death to self, to find life in Him.

The high priest of Israel was anointed with oil before he ministered *(Leviticus 8:30)*, just as our Savior, our high priest, was anointed with oil before His PASSION. As Jesus died to fulfill His destiny, we must cover ourselves with the fragrance of myrrh, the precious, costly oil of death to self, and allow ourselves to be broken vessels, to fulfill our destinies in Him.

He Led Captivity Captive

Though many spit on Him, reviled Him and rejected Him, He mercifully freed them from the bondage of sin and eternal death. *...When He ascended up on high, He led captivity captive, and gave gifts unto men. (Ephesians 4:8)*

Grave Clothes

Jesus' grave clothes were made of fine linen. *(Matthew 27:59; John*

19:40; Mark 15:46) Bound in grave clothes *(Matthew 27:59)*, He was obedient even unto death. *(Philippians 2:8)* At His resurrection, He threw off the grave clothes, so that you and I can no longer be held captive by the law of sin and death.

New Sepulcher

He was buried in the grave of a rich man, Joseph of Arimathaea, a member of the Jewish Sanhedrin *(John 19:41)*. This was a fulfillment of prophecy. *(Isaiah 53:9)* *And He made His grave with the wicked and with the rich in His death; because He had done no VIO-LENCE, neither was any DECEIT in His mouth. (Isaiah 53:9)* Jesus fulfilled this prophecy even in death, to deliver us from violence and deceit. VIOLENCE (*Strong's* 2555, chamac) means oppressor, unrighteous, unjust gain, cruelty, wrong, damage. DECEIT (*Strong's* 4820, mirmah) means treachery, guile, fraud, false.

Risen

The angel said, *He is risen, as He said. (Matthew 28:6; Mark 16:6)* Jesus conquered the strongest enemy of all, death. This is proof that He is the Son of God, the first man to ever experience death and conquer it, never to die again.

Deeper Meaning of the Gospels

Matthew: He is the King Who is obeyed (purple)

Mark: He is the man Who identifies with you (white)

Luke: He is the Savior Who took away your sins (scarlet)

John: He is the Son of God Who is worshipped (blue)

These four colors: purple, white (fine linen), scarlet and blue were on the gate that was the entrance into the outer court of the tabernacle of God. These colors were hung all around the tabernacle itself and they were all four in the veil at the entrance of the Holy of Holies. *(Exodus 25:26)* The fence surrounding the outer court and the Ark of the Covenant were made of shittim wood. This special wood did not decay, and represents Jesus' flesh which never decayed, because He rose from the dead.

Caiaphas—High Priest

Caiaphas, the high priest, was deposed shortly after Jesus' crucifixion. He killed himself in 35 A.D.

Four Signs Proving Messiah Had Come—After His Resurrection

1. The lot for the LORD's goat did not come up in the right hand of the high

priest for 40 years. Then the temple was destroyed.

2. The scarlet cord tied to the door of the temple on the day of atonement, stopped turning white after the scapegoat had been cast over the precipice. (In Isaiah it says that though your sins be as scarlet, they shall be white as snow.)

3. The western most light on the temple candelabra would not burn. This light was used to light the other lights.

4. The temple doors would open by themselves as an ominous fulfillment of Zechariah 11:1, a prophecy foretelling destruction of the temple by fire.[6]

What caused the above signs to occur? Rejection of the Messiah when He came. For almost 2,000 years the Jews have been dispersed. Now, they are gathering in their homeland, once again. The relentlessness of constant war with their neighbors is wearing them down. As the world looks for the Messiah's second coming,

THE BLOOD

Jews still look for His first. Many around the world will be deceived and embrace the anti-christ false messiah, who will offer them a false and temporary world peace, an end to the relentless wars they now suffer.

Bibliography for Part Three

1. Storms, *Jesus, The Suffering Savior*, pp. 2-3

2. Wyatt, **Discovered, Volume, pp. 95-101 (further reference from Ron Wyatt, archeologist and anesthesiologist,** through phone conversation)

3. *Parade Magazine*, Feb. 16, 1992

4. Wooten, *In Search of Israel*, pp. 103-107

5. Wooten, *Who Is Israel?* pp. 63-69

6. Brown, *Are the Rabbis Right?*, (cassette by Messianic Vision)

7. Spurgeon, *The Death and Suffering of Jesus* (general reference guide)

CATALOG: for Bree Keyton Ministries

<u>Suggested Donation</u>

BOOKS

1. *Stripes, Nails, Thorns and The Blood* $24.00
2. *Jezebel vs. Elijah* $13.00
3. *America: Repent or Perish* .... $ 6.00

VIDEOS

1. *Jezebel vs. Elijah* $29.00
2. *Spiritual Weapons of Our Warfare* $29.00

CDs

1. *Heart & Soul Surrender* (music) $16.00
2. *Healing Scriptures* $10.00
3. *Bitter-Root Judgments, Inner Vows & Soul Tie*.......... $10.00
4. *Twenty-Three Minutes in Hell* .... $ 2.00
5. *Victorious Scriptures* (two CDs) $12.00

AUDIO CASSETTES

1. *Heart & Soul Surrender* (music) $13.00
2. *Healing Scriptures* $10.00
3. *Bitter-Root Judgments, Inner Vows & Soul Ties* $10.00

4. *Twenty-Three Minutes in Hell* ....$ 2.00
5. *Victorious Scriptures* (two cass.) $12.00
6. *Advanced Spiritual Warfare* (12 part series—cass.) $40.00
7. *For the Bride: Song of Solomon, Esther and Ruth* (two cass.) $12.00

OTHER PRODUCTS
1. *Stakes* $10.00

(Please include $3.00 Shipping & Handling on all orders)

About the Author

Dr. Bree M. Keyton is the author of several books. She is an ordained minister holding two teaching certificates in English and in Speech and Theater, with certification in Missouri. She holds doctorates in Theology and in Administration and Education. She is a professor at Faith Bible College where she designs curriculum and serves on the board as Director of Research.

Bree ministers in power evangelism, brandishing a sword of steel while exercising the sword of the Spirit. Thousands have been saved, delivered and received physical and emotional healing by the awesome power of God. Bree's mandate from the LORD is to **SET THE CAPTIVES FREE!**

Bree has a CD that received nationwide airplay for several years, and she travels preaching the gospel. She teaches the Word and leads her own family worship team, which performs where she ministers upon request. She has a zeal for soul winning, healing the sick and setting the captives free. She has hosted a national TV talk show and served as a worship leader.

Before being born again, Bree traveled as a warm-up act for rock stars and had her own nightclub act. She was shot in the head, and through the miraculous intervention of the living God, she survived to tell the story and share God's great healing power with others.

Bree has appeared on *"The 700 Club,"* TBN, the National Right to Life Convention, the International Counter-Cult Conference, the National Full Gospel Business Men's Convention, and appeared on the international TV program *"It's Supernatural"* with Sid Roth. Bree has ministered in arenas, churches, music halls, prisons, malls, parks, high schools, colleges, retreats, crusades, conventions, coffee houses, and outdoor festivals.

This book serves, additionally, as a textbook for a college course, *Advanced Spiritual Warfare: Stripes, Nails, Thorns and The Blood*, and college credit is available by arrangement.

Bree Keyton Ministries
PO Box 17802
Kansas City, Missouri 64134

www.breekeytonministries.com

www.americarepent.com

God's plan was more brilliant than we can imagine! This revelatory book shows why Jesus' PASSION had to be so horrific—the beating, whipping, mocking and humiliation He suffered. Each and every agonizing moment of His PASSION, from Gethsemane to the resurrection, had purpose and significance for our lives.

Each moment of the PASSION is shown in Bree's four songs (bonus CD included), and this first offering of a trilogy of ground-breaking books on the brilliant plan to save mankind, culminating in Jesus' death and resurrection.

The Passion: What Does It Mean is a powerful expose revealing who is really responsible for Jesus' death and why. It explains the true meaning behind the crown of thorns and graphically illuminates the necessity and power of Jesus' shed blood.

Dr. Bree M. Keyton wrote the powerful truths contained in this book after the heavenly Father showed her a vision (May 1993) of Jesus receiving His stripes before He went to the cross, and spoke to her to write the four dramatic works.

THORNS—for healing in our minds

THE BLOOD—for salvation

You will be forever changed after experiencing this music and book.
Hit MUSICAL CD INCLUDED
(Coming Soon)
The PASSION: What do the STRIPES Mean?
(Book Two in Series)
The PASSION: What do the NAILS Mean?
(Advanced Spiritual Warfare)   (Book Three in Series)